My story of 10 years fighting a very evil system.

By troy-joseph: sumal

They took my driver license away 10 years ago. This is my testimony. The truth and revelence of the corrupt system between commercial contractors sharing a performance contract,

To emogene johnson smith>>BITCH-FAKE-JUDGE-FUDGE-NO-OATH-OF-OFFICE-SATAN'S-SADIST-BAAL-PRIEST-IMPOSTER-ADMINISTRATIVE-CLERK-WICKED-VILE-

& ALL-THE-REST- michael w morrissey, anne yas>district attorney and assistant district attorney, edward j doherty>magistrate. James alfred>plainville police captain, scott gallerani>plainville police sargent, julie barrett>plainville police officer, AND-WHOEVER-ELSE-HERE-INCLUDED-NAMED:

All the forementioned involved in evil corruption, the game is RIGGED !!! CORRUPTION=EVIL !!!!

these miscreants have nothing on me but FAKE CHARGES and an offer to contract !!

I have over 50 violations on them of which I can swear to under oath. But they want to cash in on some very pricey bonds and/or have me admit to being surety for a maritime lien, and/or other trix.

This fake case was expired on nov 9th 2015 by thier own statutes but they continue the extortion of blocking my driver lisence !!

massachusetts wrentham district court docket # 0957CR003036

My contact info: troy-joseph: sumal 3200 nw 62 ave, suite 30 margate, florida state. ZIP EXEMPT. 954-770-8524 antiquefineartt@aol.com

civil status= American National.

update jan 2ⁿᵈ 2020:

As this book has no table of contents because some of the information is added as it becomes known. As of today I have more evidence to prove my claim(s) that the BAR (ABA) is a CRIMINAL. They make up thier own rules and laws to protect each other is what Im about to explain.

2 days after christmas I decided to call the american BAR association to file a complaint against the fake judge, I left a message for them to call me back, today about 10;45 AM I recieved a call and was told to call another number in massachusetts> 617-728-8750, so I then called that BAR franchise and they do not handle any complaints on any BAR members in massachusetts, They told me to contact the judicial conduct comittee, and I told that woman on the phone I already did that 3 times and that man (howard v neff III) is also a criminal !!! she said theres nothing she could do, yeah I figured. !! I reported to him numerous counts of crimes from that bitch satanic judge and he did nothing !!!

so here we go folks on the roundy-round merry go round. This is the games we have and how the BAR>british mafia protects each other by making up thier own rules, its sickening.

What president is going to do anything about this ? NONE!!!! they are just puppets for the british investors of this sick corporation. If you are experiencing problems with court, or your friend or family member,,,,,,,, theres a few solutions I have provided for remedy to SCREW THEM !!!!

Getting your civil status changed is a good start !!! that way they cant pull this shit on you EVER AGAIN !!!

the game is TOTALLY RIGGED AND THIS COUNTRY SUCKS !! ITS NOT EVEN A COUNTRY. ITS ALL LIES HERE !!!

About the author

Troy-joseph: sumal grew up on new jersey territory. Dropped out of high shcool in the first quarter in the 10th grade to run away from home. In my early years my father was always buying junky houses every 4-6 months and fixing them up so I was one of the crew of slaves. I had 3 brothers and 1 sister and he surely used us all to labor on these fixer upper houses, my sister didnt do any repairs just some labor cleaning and such. The boys were meant for learning mechanical trades very early using hammers wrenches paintbrushes hacksaws caulking guns, you name it, I was gluing PVC pipe and all sorts of other things that normal children did not do; like making small engines run that did not run, then repairing and rebuilding small engines, rebuilding bicycles. Always something mechanical. By 10 I was painting trim on baseboards with very straight lines. Myuding 3 phase motor control and transformer building I felt i had a great chance of getting a job, and because I was close to 6 ft tall, I thought my chabces were very good I could make it on my own. I walked out of the classroom one snowy day and walked home, took my suitcase out from under the bed and called a taxi, went to the airport and bought a ticket to orlando florida for 64$. this was back in 1978. That was it. I might write the rest of that part in another book how I made it on my own father had me and my brothers helping him on the weekends on his houses and office buildings he painted, also working on his car and semi truck projects sanding and masking. But the abuse and beatings got to the point where my mother and us kids went to the battered womans shelter in red bank new jersey for almost a month. My picture was in the paper with the back of my legs showing almost all black and blue from the brass belt buckle on the belt. My mother went back after a month at the shelter an took us kids back home, there was supposed to be some agreement made with the lawyers that the abuse would stop. [my mother told me that my father was friends with the judge and they traded horses at the livestock auction is why he got away with it], yeah well I got tired of the beatings and the slavery so I split. I left my antique lamp collection and everything I had, my experience of 2 years of electric vocational training incl. Ive aleways had a high intelligence for mechanical trades and when I ran away I was in the process of restoring a 1966 3/4 ford flatbed truck. Ive had many jobs and experiences. At 54 years old now I have knowladge of electric wiring , plumbing, carpentry, auto mechanics, renovate houses, furniture repair and refinishing, antiques and fine art, the list goes on. Ive never spent much time in bars and TV watching so Ive always been busy doing something productive. I had some tickets before and I never until now knew this system was this way. During my 10 year experiences of fighting for a driver lisence I met a couple who had thier 4 children STOLEN by kidnappers [court & police]. I fought for 7 months to get those children back and learned quite a lot more about the system. Many documents I've prepared including affidavits, legal notices, complaints, all entered into the record and hand delivered to clerk and state attorney's office. The charges were dropped and 2 public defenders quit the case, the judge walked off the bench permantly, but then a new judge appointed himself. It was no use. I was totally drained and they would not obey the laws or thier oath of office. The judge and prosecuting attorney kept those 4 children and destroyed a family. It's a rigged game and they DEFINATLEY DO NOT play by the rules. I have the video where 6 fat overwheight cops are trying to keep under control a 12 year old girl and a 5ft 4in mother, the fat cop assauloted the mother and tasered her numerous times while cuffed and the cops drug them both like animals on the ground, there were 7 -10 police cars on the scene, and of course the "spotter" she gets 5000-10,000 for making the call, the mother and father and children stopped into the casino to use the bathroom and left thier children in the minivan being watched by the 14 year old which is well qualified to watch her syblings, it wasnt even a hot day, and then the "spotter" seen the opportunity for CHING A LING $$$$$$$$$$$$$$$$$$, this happened in 2014 and to this day the children are not with thier parents !!!!!! because they are worth a fortune to the court, [and childnet, including all others involved in the performance contract and bonds], and thats the way that goes. Very sad. Ive also in my experience have become a debt relief expert as my credit report has been cleaned up and remains all zeros with no debts. I helped one woman wipe out over 65,000$ in debt in 3 1/2 weeks. We are still friends to this day. I've studied the banking system and mortgages also over the years and more and more fraud. Lying cheating and stealing, and of course the EVIL BAR attorneys & judges help them do it !!!! Ive been to court and jail a numerous times while fighting for my right to travel freely. That didnt work out because of numerous reasons but It tought me a whole lot more experience of how the system works. this book is to tell my story and inform other Americans of what ACTUALLY is happening in these courts. I guess its on a level where if someone had absolutely NO knowladge of what really goes on with this system, its a beginning to understand, because it is only scratching the surface. It gets way deeper and complicated as now im studying more complex information. Links below for education reference.

https://www.youtube.com/watch?v=cMwaABDQGs8 subrogation videos !

Win In Court - Subrogation Update & Express The ... - YouTube

W

e

https://www.youtube.com › watch › v=cMwaABDQGs8

b

Subrogation in Traffic Court - YouTube

r

https://www.youtube.com › watch › v=JmbwEernc6Q

e

subrogation put to the test in Traffic Court. ... 8 videos Play all Maritime and admiralty law and

ueception ...Stop A Court Case - Subrogation Concept Only – YouTube *https://www.youtube.com ›*

lwatch › v=GuTFQr39Gwc* https://www.youtube.com/watch?v=rke4QqP85XU&feature=youtu.be

t

Shis evilness must be exposed also to inform others. And it it surely is EVIL because of the amount of fraud, lies and trix, lawlessness has SEVERELY infected this land of America !!! I have over 45 pounds of printouts and copys of legal notices and complaints fighting for a driver lisence which IS MY RIGHT. As you will find out,, it is a RIGHT and not a privelage. After an incident of a police arrest and the unlawful taking away of my driver lisence was a really big shock to me how this could be done and lead me into a 10 year investigation while I figured out this "sewer system" of lies. The presidents **do know** whats going on currently and over the past decades. They NEVER address this problem !!!! because it makes TONS OF REVANUE !!!!! BILLIONS even trillions of $$$$$$$$$$$$$$$$$$$.

nobody is going to "clean up the swamp" thats **nothing but a LIE.** By the way,people using thier automobile for personal travel DO NOT need a driver lisence, only those who are transporting goods or people for hire are called commercial drivers. Like a taxi driver, a bus driver, a semi truck driver who use the roadways for commerce need a lisence, and NOT a traveler, theres tons of law and proof on this subject so I might do another book to inform the people. You will find alot of truthful information on youtube and facebook, and have fun finding out the men with guns and thier statutes are going to give you a fight when you exercise this right. But there is alot of success out west CA, AZ, NV,they win in court and the police cant do a dam thing about it. Theres just too many doing it now and have support groups and the courts CANNOT win !! (look up the charlie sprinkle case, no driver lisence for 37 years).

massachusetts wrentham district court docket # 0957CR003036 fraudulent case, fraudulent police complaint, using fictitious names.

My contact info: troy-joseph: sumal 3200 nw 62 ave, suite 30 margate, florida state. ZIP EXEMPT. 954-770-8524 antiquefineartt@aol.com

civil status= American National.

Preface: My book has no table of contents, im not a professional writer and everyone wants me to buy thier program, yeah well I dont have the $$ and time for all that. This book is very understandable. If people dont want to help me ill just do it myself.

My use of satanic depictions in this book are for the reason:

people that lie continuously, people using different grammars for trickery, people that protect each others crimes, people that co-conspire against one's rights, people that destroy lives because it brings them joy, people that know they are dishonest crooks but continue to do so, people that co-contract with others to take a driver lisence for the purpose of extortion, people who violate the constitution and make up thier own rules of lawlessness !! they'll steal anything they can from you and trick you right into thier trap !!!! its clearly SATANIC !!! I've seen recent books titled "satan's court" and "satan's docket",. the fraud is staggering. There's very experienced guru researchers using the words "satanic" and "pirates" and these scumbags can go through life with thier big smiles in public !!!??

My main purpose of writing this book is to expose this "gang of criminals" and there IS NO CONSTITUTION in thier agenda, they dont even obey thier own statutes !!!And there has been numerous people asking me why I dont have a lisence for all this time, and I tell them It would take me at least 3 hours to answer that question. Of course they think fines must be paid is what the average individual would think its my fault because they get thier information from other sheople and the TV, but now I can tell them my book is online and theres your answer why I dont have my driver lisence. we're not talking just one or two frauds but every fraud you can imagine !!! its off the charts !!!!. this case has expired by the statute of limitations on nov 9th 2015 !!!! and still nobody will speak to me ?? or answer a complaint or letter ??? THIS IS CRAZY !!!!! and yes I'm still angry, very angry every day goes by I cannot use my truck to earn a living so I can take care of my needs. Theres people in my life wondering and wondering why this is still happenening and they cannot understand it. I just keep telling them this legal system is very corrupt and its not what you think it is. They have no idea,,,,,,,,,,,,,,,,,,, they think its about paying a fine or that somebody will actually speak to you and work it out, or some other reason,,,,,,,,, plus they havent researched for the years that I have,It's surley very immoral, lawless and wicked for these people (fake judge, police, court clerk, clerk magistrate, district attorney, governor, public pretender, & town hall and insurance company, and all the secretaries) too all KNOW whats going on and continue thier games thinking nobody can ever stop them, well heres a trick that will stop them but Im not going to do it because I will not enter thier thier satan's temple alone. Its too dangerous. One could say **"I demand the prosecutor certify my right to subrogation"** and do not consent to proceed.(bring friends with video cameras LOL !!) Of course they will start murmmering and try to coerce you, threaten you with jail, theyll try anything !!!! and they cannot enter a plea for you without a power of attorney either !!! [so this is a very powerful technique as there is a video I've included with the information, and this **is not legal advise** but a kindly suggestion, that should be used and spread it throughout the land to stop these creeps).They need 3 signatures to cash out thier bonds and make other securities !! this is why they keep insisting you hire a lawliar or accept thier public pretender. the judge, prosecutor, and defendant's attorney signatures are all needed so they can get the BIG MONEY !!!!$$$$ and this is what its all about. TDA and SOCIAL SECURITY account access, & bonds $$.

I've called numerous numerous times telling them I'm sleeping in my truck and having dental problems because of no driver lisence, and other hardships. They dont give a dam about anybody's travesty!!

This is not legal advise or intended for such. I am dealing with: extortionists and mafia. People who take something valuable from you and use it for extortion because they are after big money [a ransome] they disobey all law(s), they make up thier own rules, AND they refuse to communicate, they even block your phone calls, they do not return a call, they do not write back, I have only recieved one letter from a court clerk saying I must show up in thier court. Well its not a "court" and they are not government !![as the whole trick is to get you into thier forum of fraud so they can all gang up on you with thier intimidation and threats!!!] as the facts provided will prove the truth. I want to get this information out to the people to inform them of what is REALLY going on here in "America". The "tell-lie-vision" tells lies, and so does the school, so why do they teach us in school about the bill of rights and the constitution, and then we get thrown into a world of statutes and codes ?? doesnt anybody think this is strange? Why does trump even speak about a constitution when it only exists on "tell-lie-vision" it sure doesnt exist out here in "statutes-land" !!

For those of you who do not know the system was this way, this will help you understand. For those of you living in the wrentham area you might want to clean up this fake court with a class action lawsuit, maybe 10 or more people suing in a federal court might help to change this on-going fraud against the people, or at least give awareness. There are certainly more than myself that have been damaged. Probably hundreds of thousands in the massachusetts territory

A man named charlie baker has taken the responsibility of the territory of the commonwealth of massachusetts as governor when he was elected. This man **IS responsible** for all the criminal corrupt corporations operating in his territory. But he allows corruption and ignores it. These entities called "courts" and the district attorney, public pretender, police are all businesses. Charlie baker's office personel are (2 young girls answering the phone), are trained what to say and to ACT in a governmental capacity when they are NOT a branch of any government ! They are ignorant of the law(s) and refused me to a copy of this mans oath of office. I asked to speak to the Lt Governor and that wasnt possible either. So they can read this book and I dont give a dam what they do. I'm not here to lie and fabricate the truth. I say what has happened in my experience(s) while fighting for my driver license which should have NEVER been taken. These creeps they think are so smart that nobody will be able to figure out thier games. They lie like a MF all the time, they are professional **actors,** Liars, Decievers, intimidators, extortionists. They've had decades to figure out how to SCREW YOU. And theres more involved than what you think. They think they are untouchable because thier BAR member friends will protect them>>other judges and lawliars, politicians, etc etc etc etc etc, which they all stick together and DO protect each other as youll find out. If youre fighting a case now you already know what I'm saying. THEY MAKE UP THIER OWN RULES !!

The creeps need your consent to enter into contract. And they're using fictitious names, be aware and learn the truth what theyre after. It's your consent to thier contract first of all, then when they have you roped in they'll go after the bounty of bid bonds, or maritime lien, or any other type of security (CRIS) they can monetize from your consent. they'll use any trix, any means of cruel and unusual punishment or intimidation to get thier goddam money. They'll never get a dime from me and they know it. After these years passed they know I've figured them out is why now they all have become silent and refuse to even speak to me on the phone, very sad, these people smile all the time calling them self a justice system. When its a "just-us" sistim of stench dark energy pirates and sadistic creeps.

In summary: this book is about a group of people (imposters acting as government), this group of people all intertwined and mafia behavior, they all get a piece of the bounty, acting as lawless criminals and thinking they are unstoppable, they make up thier own rules and commit extortion, the leader of the territory of the commonwealth of massachusetts is governor charlie baker, and he does nothing about it. He certainly knows about it. And this is only one county. I suspect the entire state is operating the same way, as like it is across the nation like an infectious disease this system is totally fraud.

END of preface,,

You might find remedy of your case with the information provided, but tread with caution. You are dealing with devils have no empathy for any other human. There will be a revised edition as soon as I can get all my documents in order and have them scanned, much more information will be provided to reveal what has been supressed from us. **[check out SEDM.org].**

I think I have found my own remedy for this problem , It will take me months to try it out and to see the results, the slate will be wiped clean, and they can take thier fake case, fake names, and fake warrant, AND SHOVE IT !!. In my revised edition I will share the information.

I called governor charlie baker's office on nov 8th 2019. I did call a couple years back with no results, but after a 10 year case has not yet remedy I'd try again, And it didnt surprise me of the fraud and games STILL going on with manipulation & lying. **A young girl answered the phone named camilla.** I told her i wanted to report a corrupt court, and I want a certified copy of charlie baker's oath of office, first she told me the court is in a "judicial branch" and not in thier jurisdiction, ? [I wonder what branch see would say about the police and town hall], Then I had to explain to her when this governor was admitted to his office he had to swear an oath, and where is it? She had no answer and was confused, I then told her these government public officials must swear to a constitution , [either state or American constitution] and be responsible for upholding righteousness and prevent crime, she had no answer, so I told her to connect me to somebody with some knlowladge of law over 50 years old, and is the leiutenant governor available? She then connected me to another young girl, i'd say about 24-27, who also didnt know anything about the law or oaths, neither of them offered to take a message from me or offered to have anyone call me back, So is this how charlie baker trains his employees????

Good ole charlie baker, ya know folks there's such a thing called "ethics" and "morality", and a conscious of righteous actions including the persuit of justice & the protection of rights and property in his territory, but he has his office cronies trained to read a script and refuse to take messages and refuse to let you speak to anybody, they shut you down quick. Ok so now we have a man elected governor who has knowladge of felony criminals throughout the massachusetts territory and he does nothing ? This is called aiding and abetting & also accessory, sure is !! and I've only spent 20 minutes online and seen a vast amount of complaints of corruption and mafia police on charlie baker's facebook page and other sources.

 If I should witness an armed robbery, should I not call the police because its not my jurisdiction? If I should know of a fraud comitted against an elderly person, should I make believe I dont know anything about it and ignore it ? If I knew about a criminal operation that was hurting many people by violating thier rights and ruining lives, should I turn my head the other way? Especially when I had the power to stop it? Somebody explain this Governor's logic to me with his dum ass "its not my jurisdiction" excuse !! the commonwealth of massachusetts is a "field day frienzy" for corrupt criminals, because theres nobody there to stop them, either cowardly or paid off, nobody could be that STUPID not to know whats going on !!It doesnt take alot of knowladge to help a small business, like I see mr baker makes great public notice of his good deeds, and anyone with common sence can do it, the massachusetts people are really COMPLAINING ABOUT CORRUPTION, and yet he does nothing.But yet charlie baker likes to have his picture taken with sports players and a little boy at the cancer hospital, oh wow, well the facts show the scales **are heavily weighed with his wrong-doings when compared to** his hollywood acting appearances. Without an oath of office he is an imposter of office and must be registered under the FARA> foreign agents registration act. But call his office and talk to a bimbo and see where you get. LOL, they dont know anything !!

heres the "Branch" they claimed to be an executive branch of what?? Dun & Bradstreet ?? heres thier corporate listings I took a screenshot with my laptop,. Shame on charlie baker telling these girls to lie for him !!

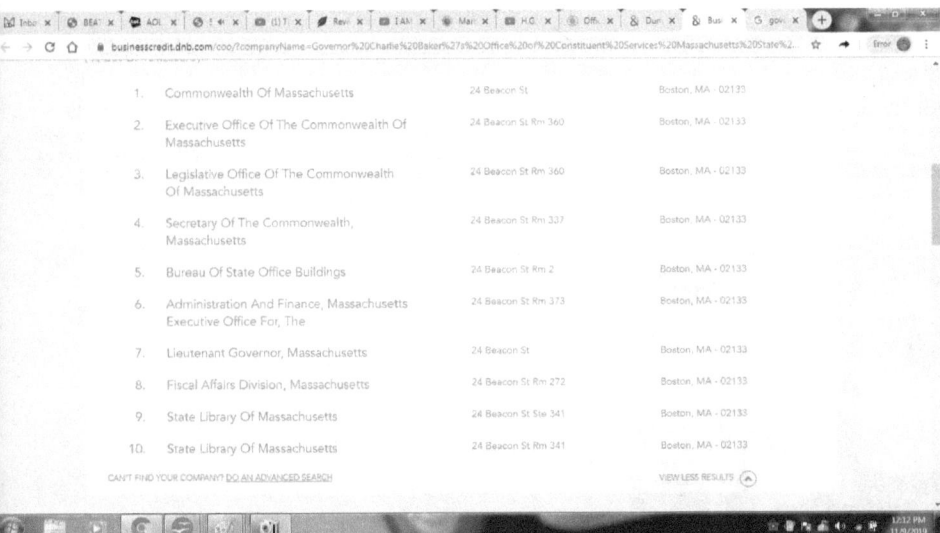

Let me tell you people I see it here in florida too, the senator's office has dum ignorant haitian woman working there, they think they're so importaqnt with thier job and they'll say anything and do anything they are trained, thier minds are like silly putty, so this camilla was acting on behalf of charlie baker's office in a capacity of legitimate government saying thier office is executive branch and the court is a "judicial branch" , claiming governor baker's office didnt have jurisdiction over a judicial branch ?? THERE ISNT NO BRANCH !!!, and the governors office isnt even a branch, either you are government or corporate, YOU CANNOT BE BOTH, its one or the other. And it's all corporations !! and WHY doesnt this man charlie baker take responsibility for the territory [commonwealth of massachusetts] of which it is his duty ?, well apparantly he's playing the role of CEO for corporate "for-profits" "commonwealth of massachusetts" and he certainly does know about the sub-franchises of the district of columbia and other corporations in his territory committing crimes of felony, extortion, fruad, and rico raqueteering. Theres many other courts besides the one i'm dealing with doing the same to other people, extortioning them and whatever else they do,The facebook page on this man is flooded with complaints !! recently i seen one saying "clean up your state with state police mafia" courts,, etc, etc, etc, .

If I should call his office back and ask for a delegation of authority from a continental congress,,,,,,,,,I already know what's going to happen, camilla will make up stories and whoever else will talk thier bullshit. I also filled out two contacts online asking questions and both are not responded,

It is a VERY SERIOUS criminal act to take away a driver license. it ruins lives. I never had the chance to go to court, not even a days time, the governor and his office employees dont give a shit about peoples rights, just thier paycheck. I'll bet charlie is taking ALOT of payoffs to turn his head the other way and ignore all these criminals, Its impossible **not to know** whats going on. Charlie baker likes to put on a show like in hollywood, meet with famous sports players and have his picture taken, or go visit a little bald kid with cancer and have his picture taken with all the smiles, this is all they can do to gain public trust is TO BE AN ACTOR !!!

I think its a fair estimate theres 100 or more criminal corporations this man knows about and he will smile about it and distract the people (with his acting and smiling), and have his very young script readers take phone calls, which are VERY

IGNORANT of any law(s). He is certainly responsible.

All BAR members protect each others crimes, BAR=british accredited registry=british mafia, that's thier oath, charlie baker's ENTIRE territory is infested with criminals and he dam well knows about it, but leaves a young girl to take his phone calls?? LOL thats really irresponsible and lacking professional accountability, the town halls, district attorney, public pretender, court clerk magistrate, and police & jails are all partaker in the same performance contract, taking thier slice of the payoff(s) he aint going to do a dam thing about it but keep smiling with his broadway acts in public

Wrentham District Court MA, fraud, corrupt, BAR MAFIA LAWLESS EVIL, IS NOT A COURT BUT A BUSINESS, BAR=British Accredited Registry=british mafia, extortion + malice, Thomas L Finigan first justice. Emogene Johnson Smith fake judge. Diane Duffey judges secretary, Michael W. Morrissey district attorney & Anne Yas assitant attny> all fraud !! Liars !! criminals. fake police report, fake case, no jurisdiction, using fictitious names, imposters with no oath of office, I do not have a contract with them. suspended my lisence 10 years ago

A BAR member will never expose a corrupt court, its not ever been done and never will. (only on very rare instances where the crime is SO OVERWHELMING), The police are trained by BAR members, I now see 4- different names [not mine] on this police incident report, they know EXACTLY what they're doing. And they agreed to use this foreign grammar? If you watch the justinian deception videos, its creepy that they teach this in schools! Like the state [teachers] are actually teaching you how to screw yourself in legal land. :((first name last name>>bullshit) The BAR creeps can steal your children, defend the cop that shoots you for no reason, cover up corrupt court activity, and definatly EXTORT you by taking your driver license. They are all criminals and think thier system cannot be figured out. But there are many like myself who have figured out thier miscreant ways of trickery, lies, and mafia criminal gangster habits. Now that the BAR creeps know I'm onto thier games they all have become silent and refuse to speak to me, but yet they will continue to keep a block on my driver lisence. This is MALICE & cruel and unusual punishment and they are VERY SICK, SADISTIC, EVIL, GREEDY Mfs !!!!!!!!!!!. they will strip everything you have until you show up in thier fake court so they can gain access to your trust estate. [everybody has one and this is what they're after]. Theres big money involved like i said. The judge [administrative clerk, satanic Baal priest has 5-7 different jurisdictions, and can change jurisdiction at any time !! It's very creepy they all smile and be nice while they commit crimes and frauds thats never ending. I dont plea to anything, and I dont need a satanic priest in a black robe tellin me my rights !! I have over 500 rights. They are private contractors looking for my consent to contract. The tickets are just a ploy to get you there. Everybody keeps asking me and wondering with 8 charges and a warrant why they dont want me when they are called? And I tell them its about bonds that were issued on my trust account is what theyre after. I would think thats a 10,000-15,000$ case [for 8 tickets] alone, if they could prove any of it, but they cant and they know it. I will NEVER go to thier fake court and I hope thousands of massachusetts residents get to read this report and KNOW whats going on in thier state. Its all over the country actually :(

It's all about BONDS and the B.A.R. attorney's bonding process. They want to liquidate us under MORTMAIN DEAD MAN LAW and make themselves the heir of our ESTATE DECEDENT. It also appears that the foreign B.A.R. attorneys want as many Americans to sit in jail/prison as collateral for a PUBLIC DEBT (debtor's prisons), a mortgage backed security for their retirement.

Oh wait. Did I forget to mention that the foreign B.A.R. mafia want to steal credits off of our BIRTH CERTIFICATE TRUST ACCOUNTS and to steal our private EXEMPTIONS in order to avoid their TAX liability under Title 26?

Masonic Court System

A Must Read - *Print it out for safe keeping:f*

http://www.ctmin.org/pdf/thecourtsystemandfreemasonry.pdf

A film about the Old Secret Knight Templar City of London, and the Jesuit 501c3 tax exempt Church Corporations that runs it.

They Controls all Masonic **Gold Fringe Flag**

Admiralty Law Courts called The **BAR** **B**RITISH **A**CCREDITATION **R**EGISTRY - They Control all **Paper Currency**

Central Banks around the world and the **US Federal Reserve Note** - A Paper Currency System Paper with Ink on it

backed by nothing is not money; it is only a money substitute called debt (Notes - IOY's) you cannot purchase

anything with debt notes and own it - **Just think about that for a while:x**

https://youtu.be/eHnwtkfX2k4

 The British Crown Corporation - The BAR - Is The Vatican
The Crown is owned and operated by the Roman Cult, and has been since 1213
British-American Diplomacy - The Paris Peace Treaty of September 30, 1783:x
https://youtu.be/8S1jz-peZ2A

4. BAR Association Exposed +
Remember - BAR ATTORNEY ESQUIREs - Write All Your Gun Laws

BAR SEWER RATS OF THE CITY INSIDE THE CITY OF LONDON MUNICIPAL CROWN CORPORATION, aka
UNITED STATES OF AMERICA, STATE OFs…, COUNTY OFs…, CITY OFs…, and DISTRICTs OF.

All co-[franchised] municipality [E] STATEs administered by the CROWN and belonging to the VATICAN

BAR - BRITISH ACCREDITATION REGISTRY

A Franchise of the Jesuit Knight Templar's Crown Corporation of England

The Tax Exempt BAR ATTORNEY ESQUIRE

Is a foreign agent and the Enabler of all the evil in America

and around the world - They have no licenses to practice their Admiralty Law

They are "fictitious legal individual entities," and are a

United Nations Satanic Private Monopoly

The BAR is the Enablers of the New World Order

Smart Meters - Agenda 21 - Agenda 2030 and much much more

All Crime is Commercial $$$$$$$$ - The World's Biggest Corrupt Legal System - A Franchise of The Crown

The American BAR Association (and its State alter-egos) has, for all intents and purposes, taken over our entire federal, state, and local governments. The legislative branch follows the advice of their BAR member advisors in the constructing of statutes. The executive branch does the same in the enforcement of those statutes. The judicial branch is literally a closed union shop in that regard. You can't be a judge unless you are BAR member and you can't practice in their courts unless you are a BAR member.

The term "BAR" is an acronym for British Accredited Registry [see comments below]. These snakes are in fact working for the Crown of England. And that is why the gold fringed flags are in the courtrooms. It signifies admiralty jurisdiction* [maritime law], which is another way of saying British jurisdiction [England is a maritime nation]. When you cross the bar in a courtroom, you are entering a British colonial forum.

The root for the term "attorney" originates in Sanskrit (the oldest known language) and its original meaning was "to turn or to twist". That meaning carried forward largely unaltered into the English language. The letter "a", when used as a word, is defined as "an indefinite article" and when used as a prefix it equates with the word "one" (indefinite article) which modifies the base word (torn) accordingly—as does the suffix "ey".

The extra "t" is added to separate the two vowels for proper pronunciation in accordance with the rules of English grammar. Thus, "a-(t)torn-ey" quite literally means "one who turns" (something).

This takes on added meaning when you understand that the legal profession in England has a number of titles (job descriptions), such as Esquire, Barrister, Solicitor, Counselor, Attorney, etc. And each one has a very specific function within that monarchial system. An English attorney's function is to see that all titles and estates properly turn over to the legitimate heirs. The closest equivalent to that function in this country would be an attorney who specializes in probate law.

It is no accident that the generic term used to describe a practitioner of law in this country is "attorney". As agents for the Crown of England, their function is to turn the sovereignty and wealth of this country back over to the Crown of England. And they have just about succeeded. So just what is the "English model" today? Here is how Black's Law Dictionary (6th ed.) defines "Inns of Court". "These are certain private unincorporated associations, in the nature of collegiate houses, located in London, and invested with the exclusive privilege of calling people to the bar, that is, conferring the rank or degree of a barrister. They were founded probably about the beginning of the fourteenth century. The principal inns of court are the Inner Temple, Middle Temple, Lincoln's Inn, and Gray's Inn. The two former originally belonged to the Knights Templar."

The key question that Mr. Blackstone asks regarding the Inns of Court is: Whose court is it? The answer he gives is, of course, the Crown of England.

Even today in England admission to an Inn is required before registration on the Bar Vocational Course. The Knights Templar is a secret society; they were the first international bankers. Today the Knights Templar is also part of another secret society, Freemasonry. Notice the use of the word "degree" in the Inns of Court definition above. The word "degree" is a secret society term which refers to the level to which the initiate has risen.

The initiate must take "blood oaths" in order to progress to higher levels of initiation. A friend of mine who was a 32 degree "Shriner" Freemason left the secret society because the blood oaths became unconscionable and repulsive to him. The blood oaths themselves imply or state that the initiate will suffer a most horrible death if he reveals the secrets of the lodge. Some men have reported being required to drink blood from a skull as part of a Masonic initiation. Many judges and lawyers are Freemasons. In fact, a very large number of civil servants, from judges to presidents, are members of secret societies such as Skull & Bones, Knights of Malta and Freemasonry.

Can we trust judges and lawyers who are Freemasons? According to the HANDBOOK OF MASONRY by Ronanyne, page 183: "You must conceal all the crimes of your brother Mason....and should you be summoned as a witness against a brother Mason be always sure to shield him. It may be perjury to do this, it is true, but you're keeping your obligations."

The following is the blood oath that Freemasonic "Shriners" take: "In willful violation whereof may I incur the fearful penalty of having my eyeballs pierced to thru center with a three edged blade, my feet flayed and forced to walk the hot sands upon the sterile shores of the red sea until the flaming Sun shall strike with a livid plague, and my Allah the god of Arab, Moslem and Mohammedan, the god of our fathers, support me to the entire fulfillment of the same."

Today the courts in America do in fact display a gold-fringed Admiralty flag. However, the judges and prosecutors of the Bar Association always refuse to reveal the jurisdiction when asked. The jurisdiction is a secret that they do not want people to know about. This means that the Bar Association is, in fact, a secret society.

On a few occasions judges have lied about their secret jurisdiction by stating that the court was under "statutory" jurisdiction.

(and there isnt any rules and procedure for a "statutory" jurisdiction !) The imposition of Admiralty jurisdiction on land was one of the primary grievances that the colonists had against King George. The first paragraph of the DECLARATION AND RESOLVES OF THE FIRST CONTINENTAL CONGRESS OF OCTOBER 14, 1774 sums it up:

"Whereas, since the close of the last war, the British parliament, claiming a power, of right, to bind the people of America by statutes in all cases whatsoever, hath, in some acts, expressly imposed taxes on them, and in others, under various pretences, but in fact for the purpose of raising a revenue, hath imposed rates and duties payable in these colonies, established a board of commissioners, with unconstitutional powers, and extended the jurisdiction of courts of admiralty, not only for collecting the said duties, but for the trial of causes merely arising within the body of a county."

FOLLOW THE MONEY: The Rothschilds and the Bank of England along with the London Banking houses ultimately control the Federal Reserve Banks in America through their stockholdings of bank stock and their subsidiary firms in New York. As Alan Greenspan stated in London on September 25, 2002: "The tie between the Bank of England and the Federal Reserve was cemented during the 1920s." Actually, that "tie" was formed even before the Federal Reserve Act was fraudulently passed in 1913.

Below written by a man on facebook : I couldnt have said it better myself !

This is an outrage that Americans have to live under fear, high treason, tyranny and oppression. We have nothing but corporate EMPLOYEES impersonating policemen, sheriffs, deputy sheriff's and government officials.

We are dealing with "ACTORS" who appear to have it on their agenda to hurt other people (for purposes of revenue, ill-gotten gains and unjust enrichment).

We are dealing with corporate gangsters (wearing costumes) in the municipalities who run their businesses utilizing fear and intimidation tactics, piracy, extortion and "force of arms" with unclean hands and dishonest, unfair dealings including dishonest services under the "color of law". What would the PUBLIC or representatives n the various State legislative office buildings have to say if you or I wanted to run a business this way in your asylum home state?

We have American Gestapo (FBI) who do not honor their purported "Mission Statement" or Title 42 §14141. We have American Nationals being railroaded into cages and "cruel and unusual slave penetentiaries" for victimless "commercial crimes" absent a corpus delicti, mens rea, acts reus or malum in se.

We have innocent Americans thrown in jail for the failure to waive Rights, maintain corporate compliance and involuntary servitude to commercial and DMV CODE, ORDINANCES, CORPORATE RULES, POLICIES and REGULATIONS. Impostors impersonating legitimate government officials are retaliating for the disobedience of Americans in the fifty-states.

It's all about BONDS and the B.A.R. attorney's bonding process. They want to liquidate us under MORTMAIN DEAD MAN LAW and make themselves the heir of our ESTATE DECEDENT. It also appears that the foreign B.A.R. attorneys want as many Americans to sit in jail/prison as collateral for a PUBLIC DEBT (debtor's prisons), a mortgage backed security for their retirement.

Oh wait. Did I forget to mention that the foreign B.A.R. mafia want to steal credits off of our BIRTH CERTIFICATE TRUST ACCOUNTS and to steal our private EXEMPTIONS in order to avoid their TAX liability under Title 26?

I do not support or agree with the deceptive trade practices of the PUBLIC, denial of full disclosure and the utter arrogance of these traitors when it comes to the inherent, unalienable and imprescriptible Rights of the American men and women in the fifty-states for these united states of America.

Court in wrentham massachusetts [wrentham district court], all fake public officials/employees, (no oath of office) district attorney and lots more. because of all the wrongdoings they've done to me and probably others, This court does need exposed for it is all fraud and lies, my experience of fighting for my driver license for the past 10 years with these people, its insanity. And my claims of mafia extortion will show relevence, plus much more the American people need to know about how diabolical this gets with thier tricks, these are professional criminals trained far beyond your paradigm can believe, you might start questioning your local public officials, courts, judges, town hall, and who ever you know that works in a courthouse. Of course theyre all nice and smiley until you ask a question they dont like !!!! for instance while the public creeps were campaining for election last year at a nearby library i asked a candidate for judge what BAR means ? And he replied it was meaning the barrister in a courtroom? Then i asked why such a large organization of legal members named itself after a piece of furniture? He did not answer me, then I showed him my information about the BAR, He said the jails are full of guys like me? I called him a british mafia creep freek,

All the smiley face creeps want a shot at the big money $$$$$$$$$$$$$$, playing custodial trustee or executor of your estate. And there is BIG MONEY INVOLVED. Tickets are just a ploy to get you into thier forum of illusion, so they can trap you and extort you. And they will use guns , threaten you with a 30 days contempt jail-time, [knowing you will lose your job, they dont give a F], and violence to do it if nesseccary! You see the name you use is where it all begins, silly as it may sound. Our mother and father called us appellates, [a given name] our surname is private property and for legal contracts upon consent. The public fool system taught us how the state wants us to use names so we could screw ourselves in the courts and wherever and whoever else in this world can screw us by using these fictitious names that are not common english, but the state BAR legislature knows this and they tell the teachers what to teach, thats real nice isnt it.

Very recently a deputy asked me my name, and I then took out a piece of paper with 13 different grammatical types of names, at that point he left and said he was in a rush to go to another call, he asked me for a state ID also and I said it identifies a DEAD entity its not me. Anyways if I do get a driver license someday I know how to fix it up real good with a tatoo artist and documents :)

you are using a name like john smith, or mary smith, and they've changed it to JOHN SMITH or John Smith, or MARY SMITH> Mary Smith, totally differnt grammar with totally different meanings !! so when they ask you "what is your name"? You should write it on paper john-smith (a man), mary-smith (a woman). [must separate given name with surname with hyphen] At that point they will get pissed off and start intimidating you and switch to other forms of trickery. You'll learn more as you read on what these names mean and thier fraudulent papers and trix they use, thier main goal is to get you into thier cortroom so you cannot escape !! the public pretender is a LIAR CREEP also !!

Such grammatical rules can only confirm that your **Christian name and all uppercase SURNAME** [troySUMAL] have no jurisdiction with each other,[this is exactly what is on the application for complaint], in a legal sense, unless "agreed" by the two parties, but if you were never aware of such hidden knowledge that deceived you into assuming that the two names were one and you entered into a private foreign contract without you being aware.

There is no jurisdiction between two separate languages appearing on one document. This is the guts of their deceptive crime: "English" and "DOG-LATIN" can not exist as one. Reference: Article: 11:147 Chicago Manual of Styles: Sixteenth Edition: Foreign Languages.

DOG-LATIN, is the language of the illiterate, it is the: LATIN-ALL-UPPERCASE-TEXT usurped into the English Descriptive text, appearing under the grammatical rules of Descriptive English Text, (ALL UPPERCASE SYMBOLIC TEXT without the hyphens) and not appearing under the true correct grammatical rules of Latin,

Chicago Manual of Styles, also states that there is no correspondence between the words and signs of any two languages, meaning, the DOG-LATIN has no jurisdiction with the written English on any instrument (Contract) unless agreed!

Article 11:147 of the Chicago Manual of Styles: SIXTEENTH-EDITION:

This is (One of the many bits of evidence) the written hard evidence that identifies the ALL-UPPERCASE-TEXT as a foreign entity, a foreign language to the English Written Text and goes on to confirm that there is no correspondence between the SIGN language and the language of the Written Text. Not only does it confirm that there is no jurisdiction between the two written styles of text, it further identifies the grammatical error in all government and Court and Banking documents relating to the grammatical rule dealing with the SIGN language relating to hyphens between signs in order to string a sentence in SIGN-LANGUAGE. One rest in relation to SIGN-LANGUAGE constitutes a stopple between the signs, whereas, one rest in written English constitutes the joinder between the two words. Two rests are needed to confirm the stopple between words appearing in written English text, whereas only one rest will cause the stopple between words appearing as SIGNS. (Article 11:147: Chicago Manual of Styles: SIXTEENTH EDITION_ See illustration below) These are also the rules Re: **Ancient Latin, being an illustrative text, meaning symbolic text or SIGN-LANGUAGE and renders a very different grammatical rule to the written descriptive English text. Such grammatical rules can only confirm that your Christian name and all uppercase SURNAME have no jurisdiction with each other, in a legal sense, unless "agreed" by the two parties,** but if you were never aware of such hidden knowledge that deceived you into assuming that the two names were one and you entered into a private foreign contract without you being aware,

GLOSSA meaning ; written by judge anna von reitz,

3. There are two reference books called similar names (sound familiar?) --- One is the Chicago Manuel of Style, a popular style guide used widely by newspapers and other publications to provide uniform guidelines and standards for reporters and other writers; it is a large reference book similar to a dictionary or thesaurus. The other is The Chicago Manuel of Styles, with an "s" which is a much smaller and more limited publication the size of a larger format paperback book, that deals with the subject of "styles" or "stiles"(British) exclusively. The most recent edition I can find is 1948, though there may be more recent editions.

Both of these publications adequately explain what the Glossa is, as does Black's Law Dictionary. The earlier versions of the American Bar Association guides to legal style and usage also plainly state that the **use of all capital letters denotes either a corporation or a dead man's estate.**

also by judge anna von reitz;

john –quincy: adams = a living American endowed with all his natural rights
John Quincy Adams = a foreign situs trust used in commercial shipping
JOHN QUINCY ADAMS = a foreign estate trust
John Q. Adams – a public transmitting utility company
John q. Adams = a public foundation
JOHN Q. Adams = a cooperative
JOHN QUINCY ADAMS = a boat or ship used in public commerce
JOHN QUINCY Adams = a commonwealth trust
J. QUINCY Adams = a slave owned by Exxon Corporation
J.Q. Adams = a foreign pauper forbidden to own land
Adams, John Q. = a taxpayer

ADAMS, JOHN Q. = a soldier
adams, john q. = a slave

There are dozens of different potential meanings that can be arbitrarily assigned to anyone's name and used to "represent" radically different entities. In a verbal conversation we can talk all day long about someone or something named "John Quincy Adams" and which john quincy adams or what kind of JOHN QUINCY ADAMS will never be known, except from the context of the conversation — but on paper the use of such a system instantly defines what or whom is being talked about — if you know the system

By the way i've seen over 20,000 youtube videos, I've researched the best of the best teachers out there and checked thier information through other sources before determining what is true, I am not just going to repeat the first thing i hear and base a belief it is true without searching many other sources, And during the past 10 years I've had no social life, I dont watch TV, I just continue my research among trying to provide for myself to keep food in my body IS all i can do for now, This is a short book and there will will definatley be a revised edition as soon as I can get settled in better living conditions and dig out all my papers and get them scanned and tons of information on this "system of fraud and mafia control".

emogene johnson smith

administrative clerk/actor/fake judge

howard v neff lll, judicial conduct

protects fake judges crimes !

Emogene johnson smith>>foreign agent of a cult. no oath of office and not bonded !!
18 USC Sec. 912, 01/03/95; EXPCITE:
TITLE 18 — CRIMES AND CRIMINAL PROCEDURE, PART I — CRIMES, CHAPTER 43 — FALSE PERSONATION;
HEAD: Sec. 912. Officer or employee of the United States.

STATUTE: Whoever falsely assumes or pretends to be an officer or employee acting under the authority of the United States or any department, agency or officer thereof, and acts as such, or in such pretended character demands or obtains any money, paper, document, or thing of value, shall be fined under this title or imprisoned not more than three years, or both. See this and this for more information.

Mafia BAR member michael w morrissey will not answer any letter, affidavit, or phone call. Co-conspiritor with emogene >fake judge, they'll take your driver license until you show up in thier fake court, caz theyre after the big $$$$$$$$$ like i said, dam little traffick ticket doent mean a dam thing to them, the BAR conjured it up as a ploy,

michael w morrissey refuses to speak to me also, as I am well capable of defending myself as it is my right, mr district attorney doesnt want to hear any law or my rights, or a fake police report, his bich secretary has blocked my calls and they are also responsible for blocking my driver lisence and continuing this FRAUD & extortion. but his people say Im supposed to show up in thier "court". I will NEVER put my liberty and safety in the hands of these miscreants, they are so evil and wicked :(

 these jerks keep telling me since 2010 I cannot defend myself and to hire a lawliar? And I keep telling them I am well capable of defending myself and amendment 6 garuntees me the right. 10 years this has now been going on with lawless criminals.

Faretta v. California, 422 U.S. 806 (1975),[1] was a case in which the Supreme Court of the United States held that criminal defendants have a constitutional right to refuse counsel and represent themselves in state criminal proceedings

edward j doherty, clerk magistrate, also a big fraud and does not respond to any mail or phone call, he is co-conspirator to extortion and depravation of rights. Extortionist fraudster also wants me in thier fake court so they can threaten and intimidate me untill I admit to being **DEAD.** theres many other games to get you into thier court, such as dog licenses, code enforcement, collecting rain water, growing a garden, oh they have lots of schemes, and they hit your TRUST ESTATE for anywhere from 10,000-75,000$ [depending on the charges, and bonds] everytime you walk in the door !!! thats why sometimes they'll continue a case for as long as they can !! AND GET YOUR SIGNATURE as many times as they can too !! [they monetize it as a security] **here is one method they use: but there are also maritime liens,,,,,,,,,,,,,,,,,,,,,,,,,**

An officer issues a citation or complaint, the bid bond. They then come looking for your corporate fiction, your shadow. They find you and take you captive (like the winged monkeys took Dorothy), since they consider you to be the fiduciary for the mindless fiction or strawman (a felon, guilty before proven innocent). They drag you before some administrative magistrate, who converts you into the surety by conning you into posting bond, a booty that he and the officers receive a portion, thereof. Which then, makes you liable for whatever performance bond is determined by the Black Robed Devil some time in the future. They steal both your wealth and your time.

Accepting RE-presentation, Appearing (Except by SPECIAL PRESENCE), **stating ones name on or for the Record, or entering PLEA are sure losers. Each of these grants jurisdiction. Never state ones 'Nom de guerre' or name, NEVER! NEVER! A case must be won prior to or at Arraignment. There are two things, which these DEVILS cannot do to their victims; they cannot arraign or sentence anyone, who is without RE-presentation. PERIOD. RE-present means to present as something other than as self.**

Once one enters, the sharks, lions and vipers are sure to pounce on their victim.

Basically, it works this way the Black Robed Devil send the Gestapo out to pickup the "Trust", "Vessel" {49 USC §§ 1176-1282 Addendum}, Transmitting Utility {UCC 10-104} or so-called "Strawman" or "TIN man". The Gestapo finds you at the appointed address, you identity or accuse self and the Gestapo seizes you as the Fiduciary. They then take you, the assumed Fiduciary, before the administrative magistrate, who CONS or coerces you into becoming the Surety. Does recording of the Commercial Paper discussed in previous paragraphs begin to make sense? He, who files first, WINS!

"...(A)n attorney [THE COURT'S JESTER] occupies a dual position which imposes dual obligations." His first duty is to the courts [THE BLACK ROBED DEVIL WHO IS GOING TO PUT YOU AWAY or EXTORT FROM YOU AS MUCH AS HE CAN POSSIBLY TAKE.] and the public [THE STATE], not the client [A FOOL'S FOOL], and wherever the duties to his client conflict with those he owes as an officer of the court in the administration of justice, the former must yield to the latter." - 7 CJS § 4. "Clients are also called 'wards of the courts' in regard to their relationship with their attorneys." - 7 CJS § 2. "Wards of court. Infants and persons of unsound mind." Which one are you? "Davis' Committee v. Loney, 290 Ky. 644, 162 S.W. 2d 189, 190." - Black's Law Dictionary, 6th Ed. ALL ATTORNEYS AND JUDGES HAVE AN ATTORNEY ON RETAINER TO REPRESENT THEM; THEREFORE THEY ARE ALL PERSONS OF UNSOUND MINDS. THIS IS MADNESS, BUT IT IS THEIR LAW

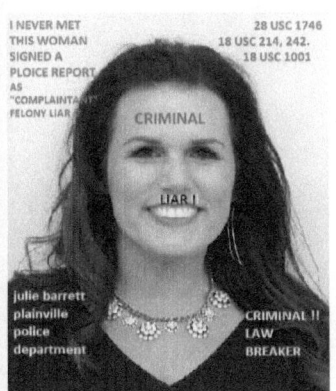

SATAN WORSHIPPERS michael w morrissey & magistrate edward j doherty, money launderer extortionist rico felon. They all need a tax AUDIT !!!

BAR= British Accredited Registry, British AristocRATic Regency british mafia liar creep criminals all protect each other's crimes !! all BAR members stick together, they all lie cheat and steal !!

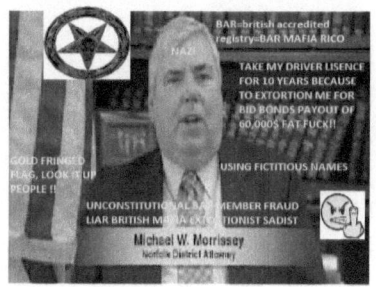

EMOGENE JOHNSON SMITH, FAKE JUDGE HAS NO OATH OF OFFICE, SATANIC SADIST, SICK-BICH, FILTHIE, EVIL, FELONY CRIMINAL, LAW VIOLATOR, BAR MAFIA MEMBER CRIME RICO SYNDICATE, LAW VIOLATOR AND TREASON, IMPOSTER OF OFFICE AND OPERATING A FAKE COURT !! . district attorney michael w morrissey thinks he is above the law, never responded to any of my complaints & anne yas assistant district attorney and never returned a phone call, the same goes for clerk magistrate edward j doherty !!!!! they dont give a dam if you are living in your car eating canned food. They only want thier big payout when you show up in thier court.

& HOWARD V NEFF III, EXECUTIVE DIRECTOR BAR MAFIA EXECUTIVE DIRECTOR OF THE JUDICIAL CONDUCT COMITTEE, PROTECTS THE FAKE JUDGE WITH NO OATH OF OFFICE,

howard v neff the 3rd, guilty of fraud, aiding and abetting, treason, conspiracy against rights, ignores felony crimes of emogene johnson smith because he claims "he has no jurisdiction over legal descisions" yeah sure, that sais it all right there you CREEP !!!

U.S. Code

1. **Title 18. CRIMES AND CRIMINAL PROCEDURE**

2. **Part I. CRIMES**

3. Chapter 43. FALSE PERSONATION

4. **Section 912. Officer or employee of the United States**

5. **U.S. Code § 912.Officer or employee of the United States**

Whoever falsely assumes or pretends to be an officer or employee acting under the authority of the United States or any **department, agency** or officer thereof, and acts as such, or in such pretended character demands or obtains any money, paper, document, or thing of value, shall be fined under this title or imprisoned not more than three years, or both.

(June 25, 1948, ch. 645, 62 Stat. 742; Pub. L. 103–322, title XXXIII, § 330016(1)(H), Sept. 13, 1994, 108 Stat. 2147.)

Wrentham District Court MA, fraud, corrupt, BAR MAFIA LAWLESS EVIL, IS NOT A COURT BUT A BUSINESS, BAR=British Accredited Registry=british mafia, extortion + malice, Thomas L Finigan first justice. Emogene Johnson Smith fake judge. Diane Duffey judges secretary, Michael W. Morrissey district attorney & Anne Yas assitant attny> all fraud !! Liars !! criminals. fake police report, fake case, no jurisdiction, using fictitious names, imposters with no oath of office, I do not have a contract with them. suspended my lisence 10 years ago

Let me share my thoughts on another subject, my book is all jumbled up anyways. So we live in a world where MANY MANY corporations are after one thing _from you._ Your consent to contract and your SS#. Have you ever noticed these collection agencies and utility companys, want your SS# for "verification"? Or automobile finance companies, or other financial institutions,,,,,,,,,,,,,,,,,,,,recently walgreens is getting your SS# when they swipe your ID for tobbaco or alcohol. Well yes they all want access to your TRUST ESTATE !!! and they are getting it. By your consent. Theyre using a form SSA-445 or other methods. And they will charge monthly or quarterly service fees or whatever other bullshit reason they fabricate and get $ $$ from your estate. To further your knowladge on this, google search "TDA minor accounts" and "age of majority" and start your trip down the rabbit hole. All medical bills are discharged through your trust estate, then they sell the information to private contractors known as debt collectors for pennies on the dollar. Thats another subject,,,,,,,,,,,,,,,,,, so anyways now the courts operate on a larger scale because they are after the big potatoes !!!! and they use a vast amount of lies and fraud, intimidation, violence, cruel punishments to get what they are after. From listening to the very well experienced teachers and from seeing the CRIS records from a court from texas I feel confident I can repeat what ive heard as non-fiction. The courts want you to admit to the fictitious name and be surety for a debt or lien, then they need 3 signatures for thier bonds, they then take 1 or more bonds and transfer it into a security(s), they are accessing both TDA and Social Security accounts for MAJOR MONEY !! 1 or more bonds may be redemable on a quicker cash-out basis. This is why they live the life of luxery and have offshore accounts. I am still researching. This is why the district attorney keeps telling me after 10 years I NEED to hire an attorney !! because theyre lacking one more signature from a lawliar that they tell me to hire, so then they can cash out on the bonds and make thier securities. they CANNOT get thier $$$$ so they have continued breaking the law and using the driver lisence for extortion.

On november 6th of 2009 I was pulled over for who knows what, the policeman told me he seen me weaving? I said i dont know what your talking about, i just left an antique auction just a few minutes ago. I gave him my rhode island driver lisence he went back to his car then 1 minute later was back at my door demanding i take a sobriety test. I agreed. So we went to the back of my truck and i did the whole routine and he was mad that i didnt screw up on anything. So I said ok were done here Im leaving. He told me to shut up because he is arresting me for OUI because my eyes were red, I told him back I wear contact lenses and keep them in for days because of my road trips dealing antiques. He insisted I take a breathalizer test and arrested me and took me to the police station.

 a fake police report was created on me, its called an "application for complaint". I didnt even see a copy of this police report till 1 1/2-2 years after the night they arrested me. I paid a lawliar to get me a certified copy from the court and OMG what is written on there !! they said i was in the median, then I almost had a head on collision, then I almost hit a gardrail, yeah right !!! thats real ludicrous, I have never heard of such BS. I included 4 pages near the end of this book.It is not even a valid police report, Its not a claim from a complaining party [man or woman], its not a verefied claim and surely not a complaint by any police officer, [it is illegal and unlawful] as "application" means request: who or what is requesting to whom? Very strange papers as I examined them. Scott gallerani is the narrative and julie barrett is the one who signed it as the complaintant? Theres 8 charges: OUI, cracked windshield, no seatbelt, expired inspection sticker, open container, no registration, lanes violation, and one more, ill have to find the application, LOL, . My sticker was expired, whoop de doo. Either somebody at the antique auction called thier pig friend because they were mad I bought out all the good stuff, or I was just a plain old victim as there are MANY. Furthermore this "application for complaint" is using 3 different grammars including GLOSSES, GLOSSA, Dog-latin, and probably legalese, of which i have learned about these grammar types over the years on various websites.[but recently has been researched and found in the chicago styles manual for writers, publishers, and authors], you may also find factual relevance information on "the justinian deception" so,,,, troy joseph sumal is my name [appellation] or troy-joseph: sumal is even more defined as a living man. On thier application they use "troy SUMAL" and "SUMAL" "SUMAL's" "Troy J. Sumal" all defines DEAD ! yeah I know what we were taught in school, but that was ALL LIES, what they teach in school about names is HOW TO SCREW YOURSELF when dealing with police and fake courts !! Very tricky indeed !! and the people need to know the traffic court can ONLY do business with DEAD entities such as legal fictions or certificated "persons". In 1862 congress re-defined person as meaning>corporation>franchise and other words of fraud taking away the inherant rights of men and women.

 this "application" is signed by a woman as "complaintant" i have never seen her before. So who is julie barrett,?what can she testify to? AND within the 3 grammar types my name isnt even on the entire THING. Its a THING because i have never seen something such a fraud in all my life, and the plainville police department has been doing this since 1905 according to thier email they sent me on public records request, The officer "julie barrett" that signed the fake police report has now left the plainville police because of a "love triangle scandal" is what the press calls it, or was it something else? Who knows because they all lie, probably drugs involved and other things theyre covering up. Heres the link, she also stated taking her cell phone was "unconstitutional"?? LOL thats funny !! how many hundreds of fake police reports has she signed as complaintant with no sworn statement, isnt that unconstitutional?

https://www.thesunchronicle.com/news/local_news/plainville-patrolwoman-sues-police-prosecutors-in-love-triangle-case/article_61b47a05-7dc8-5e04-9338-b7031e0238c9.html

BAAL-SATANIC-TEMPLE. WRENTHAM DISTRICT-COURT>> bank, foreign vessel in dry dock, corp martial military court, UCC court, theres many jurisdictions of which they can switch to anytime without telling you. Most of all they make up thier own rules and lie to your face!!! they tell you your rights? People you have over 500 rights. Think about it. And thier court uses no constitution !! the traffic court needs your consent to enter into commercial contract because theyre after big $$$, because you are a walking BANK and you dont know it. So after you admit to being the NAME (DEAD), and enter a plea, they got you right there, and not they have the power to do whatever they want and your "rights" dont mean shit to them. If you hire a BAR attorner>lawliar youre also screwed because then your re-presented as something other than yourself. Quite hard to grasp all these lies at first, but when you research this system of evil youll find out soon enough how it all fits together and see thier game. Of course they take your lisence and put you in jail,,,,,,,,,,,,,,,until you do what they want, so they can get what theyre after $$$$$$$$!, bonds or maritime lien or both, and theyll put on such a good show to decieve you.

james alfred, captain of plainville police, this is the man in charge of his department's

fraudulent police reports over the past 100 years !!. Since the "act of incorporation" of the town of plainville 1905 these fraudulent police reports have been used, and I wonder who cleverly taught these officers how to use the different grammars because they certainly know what they're doing. A police report not notarized or sworn to is called "unsworn declarations" among other,,,,,,,,,,,,,,,,,,,,like "application for complaint"> (whatever that means) this is illegal and unlawful !! , But mr police captain feels he doesnt owe anyone an explanation because he has a gun and a fuckin psycho judge to back him up with more BAR members,, so they can do whatever they want. This is the way they do business here in America.

On november 6th of 2009 I was pulled over for who knows what, the policeman told me he seen me weaving? I said i dont know what your talking about, i just left an antique auction just a few minutes ago. I gave him my rhode island driver lisence he went back to his car then 1 minute later was back at my door demanding I take a sobriety test. I agreed. So we went to the back of my truck and i did the whole routine and he was mad that i didnt screw up on anything. So I said ok were done here Im leaving. He told me to shut up because he is arresting me for OUI because my eyes were red, I told him back I wear contact lenses and keep them in for days because of my road trips dealing antiques. He insisted I take a breathalizer test and arrested me and took me to the police station. I was pissed off because he towed my truck ?!! and I wasnt even guilty of anything !!!, so we got to the police station was totally empty looked like it hadnt had a paint job in 40 years. I sat in a chair until scott gallerani [pig-cop] told me he wanted me to blow into the machine, I said fine,,,,,,,,,,,,,,,,,,,,,,,,, so he brings me into another room and has me sit beside this old contraption I felt was not accurate and probably very risky. [looked rickety and dirty] because it was a pice of shit and probably rigged, [in 1995 i had to use a breathalizer 6000 machine so i know what they look like, i did a .03 by the way, but this piece of shit they wanted me to blow into looked like it was 1980s and it was very worn and filthy, couldnt even see the name or model#] so i demanded a blood or urine test of the nearby hospital, (located 1.9 mi up the street), they refused it, I demanded to call a bail bondsman so I could get out of there but they roughed me up and put me in a cell. I then asked why I was being denied bail, and the cop (scott gallerani), told me im being charged with OUI and theres a 24 hour waiting period, and I told him back there IS NO OUI, because I told him to take me up to the hospital for an accurate blood test. He told me to shut the hell up that he is the one making the rules. I hardly slept, it was very cold sleeping on the concrete without a blanket, I did some crying, i could not believe anything like this could happen. These were like monsters without any soul, like programmed by demons. i called the bailbondsman the next day was 8;45PM or so, it costed 425$ to bail out, (and there was 3 charges), i think the bond was 10-15 thousand, the bailbondsman gave me a receipt and court papers for a 1st arraignment within 7 days. the towyard conviniently located right across the street from the police station, the owner of the towyard told me I had no more driver license and II have to get somebody to drive the truck out, and he was charging 35$ a day for storage !! he gave me his number to call when I had a driver to get it out, so my lisence was suspended in the middle of the night prior ??!!! what happened to "no right shall be infringed upon without due process of law"? What happened to "innocent untill proven guilty" ? I didnt even have the chance to go to court !! I had to move fast. I spent about an hour and a half walking all over town freezing in the cold looking for someone to drive my truck over the state line back to rhode island. I found a church and they told me the preecher wasnt there and told me where he lived. I walked about 12 blocks to his house and knocked on the door and he answered, I explained the situation and he agreed to drive my truck out of the towyard back to rhode island which was only a 20 minute ride. The preechers wife followed us till we got back the the rhoide island state line. On the way the preecher was telling me it is very sad what thier police and the system have become and he knows all about the false arrests and fraud. But he was mad they even suspended my lisence in the middle of the night and would not even let me to get my truck !! it was LOADED with antiques and collectables I had just bought at the auction.

I was totally in shock and I couldnt think fast enough how I was supposed to function as my income was dependent on using my truck. And with nobody available to drive me around within 3 states [RI, MA, CT] doing my business, my ex-girlfriend working daily job and everybody else tied up living thier own lives. And from the crooked cops and thier violation of my rights of due process, I could just imagine what they would do to me in court. I had already experienced multiple crimes they did to me and my intuition told me there's plenty more laws they would break, and I'd probably lose everything I have trying to fight this shit alone. I have no friends that could drive me around and no family. Lawliars wanted a 30,000 retainer? This was insane !! (this is because of a 3rd offence OUI/DUI of which the prior two I was never convicted. Maybe this is why the big thought I was an easy target by running my plate number. And on the papers i see 3rd offence, well ex post facto is illegal and unlawful !!! you cant take something from the past and use it to increase penalties and make conviction easier !, and probably worth a whole lot more for thier bonds !) I had to liguidate all assets ASAP and move down south because this amount of fraud was just too much for me, they acted as if they had no soul. I had to unload and load my truck numerous times moving certain items to certain places. Dropping off loads to everywhere I could think of. I had quite alot. My Ebay account was totally ruined [suspended] because I could not ship out items that had been sold. I had to bring my antique furniture in consignment shops and auctions, and all my collectables, vintage stereo equiptment, had to go immediatley to an auction I knew the owner and I could trust him. I told my antique dealers and auctioneer[s] what happened and told them I have to leave to florida till I sort this out, they could not believe it either what happened. So I chose to move to florida. I figured at least i'll have some checks coming in the next month or so while i try to get my life back.

I still had a full truck of merchandise so I found a couple of roadside flea markets along the way to make some $$. In south carolina I met a man named jean maxx, nice hatian man, . His truck broke down at the home depot parking lot and we camped out there for about 8-10 days looking for a fuel injector pump for this diesel dumptruck which was a difficult one to find used. We used my truck during the time it took to get his truck fixed, I told him I had no more lisence so we both had to watch the mirrors for pigs, because we didnt want any truble. So we managed driving around alot to junkyards and it was quite a job getting his truck back on the road. He is one smart mechanic i must say. lol, old dumptruck with a full load of scrap metal towing a little suv. I took a picture with my camera early one morning.

Jean maxx gave me gas money to follow him to miami incase he broke down again and said I could stay at a friends house. So I did. I arrived at "opa locka" just north of miami on the 22-25 of nov, 2009,. I met a nice woman called sister mary, she said i could park my truck on the side of her house and stay in it untill i get my florida lisence. I had a wonderful thanksgiving with them. On the next available weekday I went to the DMV expecting to get my florida lisence, I couldnt because it was BLOCKED by massachussets !! I have never heard of such a thing !!! take away a driver lisence without even going to court ? And then block it in the whole country ? This was crazy !!!. I then knew the system had a severe problem, very severe. I was into a severe shock my life had just been destroyed by criminals, I was ignorant back then but now after 10 years of research I know what its all about folks, its really sickening what has become of this legal system called "just-us". and to this day the court>>judge, state attny, public pretender, court clerk, including diane duffey [judges lobby secretary], WILL NOT RESPOND TO me and have blocked my lisence all these past years JUST LIKE A GODDAM RICO MAFIA EXTORTIONIST, these people are sadistic evil to the core !!! and by the smile on that fake judges face she really gets off on hurting others, . And by the look on howad v neff's face he is just downright rotton, [I wrote to him 3 times reporting this judges dishonor and criminal acts], looks like he made a pact with some very wicked spirits and his time is coming and he knows it,. As this storie continues of this nightmare, I am not the only one therye doing this to, and I'll show relevence to my words below of what I claim is true and the FRAUD of the entire system and their trix, this is still so shocking to this day the more i find out , and this court>judge & state attny will not respond because they know im onto thier game, they will just continue what theyre doing because they think their untouchable, Recently I have called diane duffey lobbyist judges secretary, she tells me rules like mafia, theres no law or fact in what this woman says, she pulls it out of thin air, and she does not answer an email with the simplest questions, like "wheres my summons"? "wheres my warrant"? "does your court want me>the man, or a person"? "Wheres any claim whatsoever" she replied they dont have to show me nuthin,I also called the clerk of the court who laughs over the phone, and I said "here i am come get me with your fake warrant", she replied thats up to the police, and I replied the burden of proof is on you people with your fake claims, so honor your warrant,, and she said it was up to the police to come and get me, so i called the police and emailed them in wrentham MA, and they refused, over the past 8 years this wrentham court and police has been notified many times by the police, court, and sheriff of broward county florida, and the reponse was "they dont want ya"

So heres the game folks, therez alot of $$$$$ here at stake, alot more than tickets, and the BAR members KNOW all about it because they all get a piece, and it gets down to extortion, evil dirtiee rotton wicked EXTORTION !!! bid bonds, performance bonds, and maritime liens are 5 and 6 digit numbers, and CRIS>court registry investment systems. Its one of the four mentioned or numerous, especially with 8 charges, this is why they have stripped everything away from me, my ability to support myself with income, my cost of health, my freedom of travel, my social life, loss of friends, loss of 10 teeth, and ya know what? They really dont giv a FUCK. this is what im dealing with, Includes>> a town hall board of directors and town administrator, and thier secretary, a police department, 2 insurance companies, state attorney, clerk magistrate of court, public pretender, a crooked judge and more, every goddam one of them are the same level of EVIL, I have copies of complaints and emails on most of them, Its really staggering that I report[ed] this fraud and treason to many people now and they all are recieving thier paycheck and kickbacks is what they seem to protect, FUCK MY RIGHTS AND AGREE WITH TREASON AND CIMINAL ACTIVITY !!, I'll provide a list of names and thier employment involved in this criminal activity as they are all accessories, this is the way it is here in America, very very sad, and they go to church and go through life as hipocrytes,

town of plainville MA, creator of it's "municipal police"

After few a years passed [im speaking of early 2017 now], and I have a better understanding of this "system", I had no response from the court so I decided to approach this problem from a different angle as I found out the town administrator and board members was responsible for its creation of thier municipal police

So I begin by contacting the town hall of plainville massachusetts and speaking with a secretary drusilla proctor who seems very nice and polite. I begin explaining about the false arrest, the suspension of my driver lisence and the civil rights violations among the false police report ["application for complaint"]. She told me to write my complaints and mail them in to the jennifer thompson town administrator and to thier police dept. I did that and many complaints were sent by certified mail and email to drusilla. I then made a public records request and found out thier police report/applications were created in 1905, this thing called "application" which is totally illegal and unlawful. I began calling the police and questioning them only to find the dispatcher totally brainwashed by statutes, other police including scott gallerani and the captain refused to call me or respond to any complaint I sent to them. Drusilla the secretary after over 5 months of communication LIED to me over 30 times. Everything she said she would do, she DID NOT do, many times said she would call me back with information and did not. I never recieved any response from jennifer thompson the town administrator or any board members.(selectmen) I saved all email communication and all complaints I mailed. At this time I was homeless, very sick, and living on can food basicaly , losing more teeth from depression and financial neglect. I told that to drusilla also, the nice sweet old lady that tells MANY LIES. At this time in my life I had to give it a break because it was draining me. I had been sick for over 3 1/2 months and the doctor at walgreens could not determine my ilness so she put me on a medication very similar for malaria. I did not get better untill another 6 weeks, and I decided from there not to make any more complaints or actions of severe emotional stress, so just some research here and there. I was letting it consume me WAY too much.

Im back now on nov 2019, and have decided to write this short book . After trying again to make communication with "them" to resolve this matter and the continuos games and lies, I've had enough with these CREEPS !! They do not play by the rules and are EVIL. I will speak to media if possible and will continue to expose the wicked ones. This rico crime

"Kangaroo Court": Origins of the Term and Examples of its Application by the U.S. Supreme Court

Black's Law Dictionary

Fifth Edition:

Kangaroo court: Term descriptive of a sham legal proceeding in which **a person's rights are totally disregarded** and in which **the result is a foregone conclusion** because of the **bias** of the court or other tribunal.

"when acting to enforce a statute and its subsequent amendments to the present date, the judge of the municipal court is acting as an administrative officer and not in a judicial capacity; courts administrating or enforcing statutes do not act judicially but merely ministerially....but merely act as an extention as an agent for the involved agency---but only in a "ministerial" and not a "discretionary capacity..." Thompson v. Smith, 154 S.E. 579, 583: Keller v. P.E., 261 U.S. 428: F.R.C. v. G.E., 281 U.S. 464 [emphasis added].

It is the accepted rule, not only in the state courts, but, of the federal courts as well, that when a judge is enforcing administrative law they are described as mere "extentions" of the administrative agency for superior reviewing purposes' as ministerial clerk for an agency..." 30 Cal 596: 167 Cal 762.

"...judges who become involved in enforcement of mere statutes (civil or criminal in nature and otherwise), act as mere "clerks" of the involved agency..." K.C. Davis, ADMIN. LAW, Ch. 1 (CTP. West's 1965 Ed.)

*West's Encyclopedia of American Law

Edition 2

Kangaroo Court: [Slang of U.S. origin] An unfair, biased or hasty judicial proceeding that ends in a harsh punishment; an unauthorized trial conducted by individuals who have taken the law into their own hands, such as those put on by vigilantes or prison inmates; a proceeding and its leaders who are considered sham, corrupt, and without regard for the law.

The concept of kangaroo court dates to the early nineteenth century. Scholars trace its origin to the historical practice of itinerant judges on the U.S. frontier. These roving judges were paid on the basis of how many trials they conducted, and in some instances their salary depended on the fines from the defendants they convicted. The term kangaroo court comes from the image of these judges hopping from place to place, **guided less by concern for justice than by the desire to wrap up as many trials as the day allowed.**

Application by U.S. Supreme Court:

*The term is still in common usage by defendants, writers and scholars critical of a court or trial. The U.S.

Supreme Court has also used it. In Re Gault, 387 U.S.1, 87 S. Ct, 18 L. Ed 2d 527 (1967), a case that established that children in juvenile court have the right to due process, the Court reasoned, "Under our Constitution, the condition of being a boy does not justify a **kangaroo court**." Associate Justice William O. Douglas once wrote, "Where police take matters into their own hands, sieze victims beat and pound them until they confess, there cannot be the slightest doubt that the police have deprived the victim of a right under the Constitution. It is the right of the accused to be tried by a legally constituted court, not by a **kangaroo court**".(Williams   v. United States, 341 U.S. 97, 71 S. Ct. 576 95 L.Ed. 774 [1951]

Whenever a Judge is dealing with a Statute (always) the Judge is NOT a Judge, but is actually a (bought and paid for) Clerk masquerading as a Judge, and operating in their private capacity. Clerks masquerading as Judges who are operating in their private capacity cannot do anything judicial like issue orders or warrants, and if they attempt to do anything judicial it is a fraud and a nullity, which means it is a kangaroo court. "Kangaroo court. Term descriptive of a sham legal proceeding in which a person's rights are totally disregarded and in which the result is a foregone conclusion because of the bias of the court or other tribunal." Black's Law Dictionary, 6th Edition, page 868

These so-called courts can ONLY do brutum fulmen VOID JUDGEMENTS: "An empty noise; an empty threat. A judgment void upon its face which is in legal effect no judgment at all, and by which no rights are divested, and from which none can be obtained; and neither binds nor bars anyone. Dollert v. Pratt-Hewitt Oil Corporation, Tex.Civ.Appl, 179 S.W.2d 346, 348. Also, see Corpus Juris Secundum, "Judgments" §§ 499, 512 546, 549. Black's Law Dictionary, 4th Edition

ministerial officers are incompetent to receive grants of judicial power from the legislature, their acts in attempting to exercise such

powers are necessarily nullities. Burns v. Sup., Ct., SF, 140 Cal. 1

These so-called courts are actually pirates engaging in commerce for their Roman Cult handlers looking for somebody to enslave under

their satanic law merchant

The best way to deal with them is to get them to admit that the constitution does not apply, or that common law does not apply because

when they do that they are telling you that it is not a court, but is instead a commercial transaction.

When you start to point out that is actually happening, they will probably throw you out of there, or you can tell them that you are leaving,

but it is better to get them to throw you out, because if they throw you out, it is less likely that their PIGs (Persons In Government who

intend to perjure their oaths) will be looking for you.

Three Features of a Kangaroo Court

Court proceedings that lack the due process protections people associate with courts of law have earned the name "kangaroo court." The term has been in use since at least the 19th century, but it is difficult to pinpoint an exact source for it or to determine why its name includes a reference to an animal native to Australia.
As a general rule, a kangaroo court is any proceeding that attempts to imitate a fair trial or hearing without the usual due process safeguards including the right to call witnesses, the right to confront your accuser and a hearing before a fair and impartial judge. Kangaroo court proceedings are usually a sham carried out without legal authority in which the outcome has been predetermined without regard to the evidence or to the guilt or innocence of the accused.
Referring to something as a kangaroo court usually carries with it a negative inference because of the manner in which they are conducted. Here are three features of a kangaroo court that set it apart from normally accepted principles of fairness and justice.
Applying laws retroactively
Since the outcome of a kangaroo court is a foregone conclusion, one method of ensuring that a person will be found guilty is to create laws and apply them to past behavior. Ex post facto laws criminalize past conduct that was not illegal when it was performed. The benefit of ex post facto laws to those conducting a kangaroo court is that a conviction is assured.
Ex post facto laws are a violation of the U.S. Constitution. They take away a person's right to know in advance the type of conduct that, if performed, will violate a state or federal criminal law. Removal of this most basic due process right is a characteristic of a kangaroo court.

Lack of impartial judges

Because the outcome is predetermined before any evidence is presented, kangaroo court proceedings are presided over by a judge or panel of judges that is partial toward the prosecution. Judges during a trial in a kangaroo court usually limit or obstruct efforts by the accused to present evidence or witnesses favorable to the defense while placing almost no restrictions on the evidence prosecutors are allowed to present.

The fact that the judge in a kangaroo court is part of the sham process, the punishment inflicted upon the defendant generally exceeds what might normally be justified based upon the conduct of which the defendant was accused and convicted. Harsh and severe sentences are common in a kangaroo court.

Absence of the most basic constitutional rights

The right against self-incrimination, the right to cross examine witnesses and the presumption of innocence are lacking in a typical kangaroo court. Constitutional safeguards would stand in the way of a kangaroo court reaching its predetermined result. In some instances, limited cross examination of witnesses and other fundamental due process rights might be allowed to the defendant to conceal the true nature of the kangaroo court.

JAIL

I've been to jail more than a few times while trying to make a livingin florida and got busted for a number of reasons, you could imagine fake lisence plate sticker, etc etc etc etc, driving with no lisence, whatever. But while in the jails i hear the testimony from people is staggering whats happening !! and i'll say that 80% of the people in jail DO NOT belong there !! the traffic ticket business is BIG PROFITS and the BAR members dont give a "F" what you may suffer. I'v heard guys getting a divorce, homes being lost because of no $$$ to pay mortgage, tools and valuables being pawned to pay fines and probation payments, losing your apartment or car, losing your job, being homeless and not having food. it doesnt matter to the fake court or BAR, what you may lose, theyll take everything you have besides what youve lost ! The whole raquet i think is bringing in 20 billion a year in florida, and the politicians DO GET THIER CUT. You'll see below a court in dallas TX is showing *469 million a month, and 29 millionper week ?? Many millions and hundreds of thousands being transfered on a daily basis.* **from adolescent cases, thats enough tangible evidence for me to believe whats happening, its one of thier biggest secrets and they hide it well. Bid bonds, performance bonds and maritime liens, This is what the experts are saying and I believe them, They have much more time into research like 20-50 years experience, and theyre all saying the same thing, you may check Anna von reitz online and see the truth, I know she wouldnt mind mentioning her website.**

Case Monetization (CRIS Report) - AntiCorruption Society

https://anticorruptionsociety.files.wordpress.com › 2011/01 › case-monetiz...

1.

DISTRICT **CASE** NUMBER. D04SCX 2185-CV-1049. D05TXE 1 :00-CV-621. D05TXE 1 :00-CV-621. D05TXE 1 :00-CV-819. D05TXE 1 : 00-CV-819. D05TXE …

attemps to get copy of judges oath and updates nov 5th 2019. I received a callback from diane duffey judges lobbyist secretary on 9/24/2019, she left a message where to call for judges oath of office, [She said she spoke with the presiding justice and he suggested that I contact the administrative office in boston where all records are kept at the edward w brooke courthouse located on 24 new chardon street boston 02114], I did call a few days later to 617-788-8810 to the administrative dept of edward w brook courthouse located on 24 chardon street boston, I was connected to a young man who told me this "emogene johnson smith" has no oath of office and was appointed by another judge. I recently made a lot of phone calls yesterday nov 4th, because I have a list of people that I want thier oaths, AND they give me the run-a-round, !! different offices in boston, called the administrative twice and she told me to look online at the MA constitution the judges oath is right there ? And i kept tellin this DINGBAT i want the certified copy on paper, i want to see the judges oath of office, she then gave me suggestions of which I have already tried, these creeps make it almost impossible !!! its intentional, they know dam well what theyre doing, I wonder how they hide thier actions from thier children and relatives? Most of them sure arent on facebook because there would be TOO MANY COMPLAINTS exposing them and they know it, yeah they hide. Initially i was told by the attorney general and norfolk county to request it to the town or city, I already did that , mailed in the request to the wrentham clerk [via public records request], and they sent me back a letter with my 1$ saying they cannot provide the oath of office for emogene johnson smith. then after 5-6 hours more of research was directed back to diane duffey, [judges secretery], then still continuing, i have no results, but thier lies and games, it is STAGGERING that this place is called freedom and liberty !!! I see nothing but

CRIMINAL MAFIA,!! so I gave up on getting any oath from anybody !!! After 7-8 weeks of numerous attempts with emails phone calls and one public records request mailed in.............. I still cannot find an oath of office for this criminal judge !

Here are my phone records just for boston and wrentham and governor's office [charlie faker], including district attorney, wrentham court clerk, norfolk county comissioner and the secretary of state. I see alot of other phone calls to washington DC and new york. I copied the record for the past 90 days.,,,,,, I made so many phone calls trying to get information from circus pranxters, **it should have taken one phone call to get an oath of office,** plus charlie baker's office totally ignorant of everything did not help, theres no oath of office for him neither.

617-728-8891 11/14 10:18 AM 11 mins, 617-728-8750 11/13 12:32PM 3 mins, 617-338-0500 11/13 12:29PM 3 mins, 508-695-2611 11/11 12:27PM 1 min, 617-725-4005 11/11 6:41AM 1 min, 617-735-4005 11/08 9:45AM 12 mins, 508-384-3788 11/05 7:34AM 3 mins, 508-384-8142 11/04 8:51AM 5 mins, 617-788-8810 11/04 8:45AM 9 mins, 617-557-1114 11/04 8:35 9mins, 617-788-8810 11/04 8:26AM 1 min, 508-384-8142 10/25 10:47AM 2 mins, 617-263-6800 09/24 3:01PM 3 mins, 617-788-8810 09/24 10:27AM 9 mins, 508-384-8142 09/24 7:48AM 3 mins, 508-384-3106 09/23 2:06PM 4 mins, 508-384-3106 09/23 2:02PM 1 min, 617-727-2200 09/10 10:18AM 5 mins.

U.S. Code § 3331.Oath of office

U.S. Code

Notes

prev | next

An individual, except the President, elected or appointed to an office of honor or profit in the civil service or uniformed services, shall take the following oath: "I, AB, do solemnly swear (or affirm) that I will support and defend the Constitution of the United States against all enemies, foreign and domestic; that I will bear true faith and allegiance to the same; that I take this obligation freely, without any mental reservation or purpose of evasion; and that I will well and faithfully discharge the duties of the office on which I am about to enter. So help me God." This section does not affect other oaths required by law.

(Pub. L. 89–554, Sept. 6, 1966, 80 Stat. 424.)

I then called the district attorney's office numerous times to be lied to and my simple question[s] not answered, like; "who is handling the case of 0957CR003036"? , they refuse to answer the question and they tell me i NEED to hire an attorney, i replied "ammendment 6 garuntees me the right of self-representation" then they got mad and hung up on me, mckaskle vs. Wiggins 465 US 168, 1984 is case law also that nobody has to get any lawliar, because they ARE ARE LIARS AND CROOKS, ive only contacted over 250 lawliars in the past and 100% FRAUD is what they are, its BAR=british accredited registry, British MAFIA, and they are surely a mafia gang,

So I called back the district attorney again this morning nov 5th, and spoke to a supervisor in the wrentham location, he said theres a warrant, and i said i know, "well here i am" "come and get me" I then again asked him for the name of the state attny thats handling the case, he refused to answer and hung up on me, I then called back the norfolk county DA and the secretary told me she would connect me with megan cronin [administrator], and she told me megan cronin the administrator was able to tell me who is handling this case, so she connected me and I left a message for her to call me back, today is nov 6th, no call back, so i called again this morning on nov 6th numerous times and the secretary was blocking my call. No answer whatsoever after 9 calls. I then had my friend [lily] call and the secretary did answer and told lily to also leave a message for megan cronin, and no call back today. Lily also called the court clerk and was told that there is no attorney assigned as it is a "warrant status" . Well gee whiz just a few years ago I was told "anne yas" was in charge of the case, i just wanted to check and make sure. But now they lie and avoid me, I have written affidavits to anne yas and never recieved a response. The law says silence is acquiescense, fraud and guilt, but they make thier own law,, the law also says this case has been estopped like 8 times already because they never responded to anything, they are mafia.

so i left a message and we shall see what happens next, from so far we see these are all criminals, by the way , **diane duffey the judges secretary I asked for a copy of the warrant or supbeona or summons, and she replied "we dont have to show you nuthin"?** Yeah because its not a court bitch !! its a rico business operated by imposters acting as public officials>> BAR MAFIA CREEPS *(now is dec 2 > no call back from megan cronin,)*

Jun 25, 2019 - **Estoppel** is a **legal** principle that precludes a person from alleging facts that are contrary to previous claims or actions. In other words, **estoppel** prevents someone from arguing something contrary to a claim made or act performed by that person previously.

Res Judicata>they refuse to answer to jurisdiction also

[Hagans v. Lavine 415 U.S. 533], There is no discretion to ignore lack of jurisdiction. [Joyce v. U.S. 474 2d 215]; The law provides that once State and Federal jurisdiction has been challenged, it must be proven. [Martin v. Thiboutot 100. S. Ct. 2501 (1980)]; *Jurisdiction can be challenged at anytime, and *jurisdiction, once challenged, cannot be assumed and must be decided. [Basso v. Utah Power & Light Co. 495 F.2d 906,910]. Yeah they do not have any jurisdiction either acting as public officials but actually running a human trafficking business, I dont have any contract with these creeps and they continue to use extortion because they are after the big patatoes $$$$ like maritime liens and bid bonds, we'll get into that soon enough. When they know your onto their games, it gets worse, they become more evil and rebellious, thats why they need to be exposed !! I challenged their jurisdiction in 2013 , and they never responded

PUBLIC HAZARD BONDING OF CORPORATE AGENTS: All officials are required by federal, state, and municipal law to provide the name, address and telephone number of their public hazard and malpractice bonding company and the policy number of the bond and, if required, a copy of the policy describing the bonding coverage of their specific job they are performing. Failure to provide this information constitutes corporate and limited liability insurance fraud [15 USC] and is prim a facie evidence and grounds to impose a lien upon the official personally to secure their public oath and service of office [18 USC 912].

Fake judge emogene johnson smith has NO oath of office and no bond, This witch is supposed to be registered under the FARA, foreign agents registration act of 1938, she isnt registered either, The statute of limitations passed on this case on nov 9 2015, it is EXPIRED, fuck that too, right? More and more crimes,

STATUTE OF LIMITATIONS ON MISDEMEANORS>TRAFFIK TICKITS:

Code Section	Ch. 277§63
Felonies	Murder: none; robbery, intent to rob or murder with dangerous weapon: 10 yrs; rape, assault with intent to rape, rape/abuse/assault of child: 15 yrs.; others: 6 yrs.; indecent assault on child, on mentally retarded person, rape/abuse/assault of child, kidnapping of minor, sexual offenses such as drugging for sex, enticing for marriage, inducing minor into prostitution, lewd and lascivious behavior or acts, dissemination of harmful matter to minors, exhibiting nudity, or crime against nature: when victim reaches 16 yrs. old or violation is reported, whichever is earlier
Misdemeanors	6 yrs.
Acts During Which Statute Does Not Run	Tolled when defendant is not usually and publicly resident

General Laws Part IV Title II Chapter 277   MGL massachusetts general law

Section 63: Limitation of criminal prosecutions

An indictment for any other crime shall be found and filed within 6 years after such crime has been committed. Any period during which the defendant is not usually and publicly a resident within the commonwealth shall be excluded in determining the time limited.

Misdemeanors	6 yrs.
Acts During Which Statute Does Not Run	Tolled when defendant is not usually and publicly resident

This "wrentham district court" is a business and a bank!!! you look at the definition and tell me what the fuck im dealing with here, do you see the words "justice" or "constitution"?

I dont have any contract with these CREEPS!!!, as found on Dun & Bradstreet identified as a "Governmant Sector" then wikipedia definition of "Government Sector" then somebody for the law science group on facebook gave me his interpretation of this satanic place thay call a "court" . Impersonating a public official is also a crime !!,FRAUD FRAUD AND MORE FRAUD,

I also filed a complaint with the OIG office of Attorney general and they denied my complaint because they claimed the wrentham court is not a business, and I proved it was !! I then called

these stubborn-ass criminals and argued on the phone proving them wrong and they still insisted this "court" was not a business, Recently I found a case by Rod Class from NC that a judge admitted on record the lower courts are ALL sub-franchises of the District of Columbia,

THEY ARE ALL A BUSINESS !! including the police, & district attorney. just look it up on Dun & Bradstreet,

How are they getting away with this for so many decades? I'll get to that: more sick minded evilness, word semantics, smoke and mirrors, lies, and the BAR mafia gang of felony rico criminals all going to be exposed here in this report,

here is thier court below;--------------------------------

- Perspectives
- Solutions
- Products
- About Us
- D U N S Number

Search Companies, Content, Industries

SEARCH THE DUN & BRADSTREET DATA CLOUD

wrentham district court

Search by:
Company Profiles
Site Content
Industry
Home
>
Business Directory
>
Company Search

Search Results in: Company Profiles
Showing 1-1 of 1
INDUSTRY
LOCATION TYPE
COUNTRY
SALES REVENUE

- Judiciary Courts of The Commonwealth of Massachusetts
Norfolk County District Court/Wrentham Division

Business Credit ReportsEmail D-U-N-S Number

Government Sector
Branch
Wrentham MA United States

So this is a court? Really?

General government sector - Wikipediahttps://en.wikipedia.org › wiki › General_government_sector
The general government sector includes all institutional units whose output is intended for individual and collective consumption and mainly financed by compulsory payments made by units belonging to other sectors, and/or all institutional units principally engaged in the redistribution of national income and wealth. *[where are the words>justice and constitution]?*

Interpretation by a member of the "law science library" on facebook
It's using colored language to disguise that it's making a market to redistribute credit from the pockets and accounts that were first injected into the national economy, bypassing the inferior government sectors intil these city, town, or state can capture names of the recipients who did receive the injected credit, then hold the names against the federal institution for ransom.

Ma·fi·a
/ˈmä

1. an organized international body of criminals, operating originally in Sicily and now especially in Italy andUS and having a complex and ruthless behavioral code.
   - any organized group using extortion and other criminal methods.
   noun: **mafia**; plural noun: **mafias**
   - a closed group of people in a particular field, having a controlling influence.
   noun: **mafia**

*Behavioral patterns of the court: take away something extremely valuable to me, have no right to do so, they do not honor or follow any laws or even their own code[s], they do not answer any mail, will not answer questions, voilate the constitution and other laws, violate my rights, because they want the $$$$ $$$$$$$ of which they refuse to give disclosure, and they will lock you up until you play their "name game" and they leech you for everything you have, They lie cheat and steal! They claim to be a court but are a business>proven FACT, they impersonate public officials and smile all the time. Yeah this is definatley a mafia. So what are they after ? Well folks as strange at it may sound [and you may search youtube for more information including judge anna von reitz and kurtis kallenbach] they want me to admit to being surety for a maritime lien on a deceased infant, or maybe admit to the fictitious name which would mean that I am dead so they can cash in those bid bonds for 5 digit numbers, or some other trick !! the fake judge can use up to 6-7 jurisdictions and switch jurisdictions on you at any time !! they use 3 types of grammar that I know of , legalese, GLOSSES Glossa , and Dog-Latin. They are a business and wanting to contract with you, they do it by intimidation and threats of jail and other cruel methods while the fuckin public pretender works for them and not you thats twice as bad a deception !!! these are all BAR MAFIA MEMBERS and they stick together and protect each other's crimes, how much $$ are we talkin about? My estimation is 60,000 +++, because the fat pig wrote me 8 tickets, so this is why they want me so bad in their fake court, and I garuntee if I dont play their game they will keep me locked up until I do, I aint no fake name, the entire police report is a fraud, everything is fraud, and they sure do love those paychecks and kickbacks, even the town hall gets a cut, it's called the "JUST-US" system. And there isnt no DOJ FBI OAG or US Marshals going to do anything about it but sweep it under the rug, they are all BAR members, state rep, governor, senator, etc etc etc etc etc, all BAR MAFIA, they dont give a dam,
These creeps DO NOT have any empathy for any other human, they are sick! And most are sadistic. They destroy lives, steal property, extort money, cause severe emotional damage, And cruel and unusual punishment and the BAR members are the root of this satanism,the ones that wear the black robe are satanic priests. They can change into an ecclesiastical jurisdiction. When you mention the constitution they get mad and threaten you with contempt and or jail time, when you quote the law or stand up for your rights the black robe Ba-al priest will order you a mental evaluation by their doctor [gang member]
there are 1% or less of the population that fight their cases and I am one of the few that is fighting, the ones working within the system are sworn to oath or just choose to keep silent because they prefer the paycheck, recently a woman that works for the miami police told me about the court "be careful because they do trick you" and she claims to be a christian?
So the ones that ACT like mafia ARE mafia, plain as day !!*
emogene johnson smith>fake judge and all clerks
edward j doherty>clerk magistrate
michael w morrissey>district attorney
anne yas> assistant district attorney.
Plainville MA
town administrator, jennifer thompson
clerk, ellen m robinson- recordkeeper, secretary/assistant drusilla proctor
selectmen> robert rose, matthew kavanah, george sutherland

chairman> bruce cates, vice chairman> philip hoagland
james alfred plainville police chief, scott gallerani, & julie barrett guitly police who created a fraudulent "application for complaint"
All these I have complained, and received NO response.

As 4 months ago from now nov 18th 2019, I have searched with great effort to find the particular agency of which to file a complaint against a judge's conduct. All information leads to howard v neff III, of the judicial conduct comittee. This is creepy, as I called the first time and the secretary told me "what did the judge do? Yell at you"? And I replied the judge has done a whole lot worse like a string of felony crimes. And the secretary told me to write my complaint to howard v neff, which I did. The secretary told me also this traffic case should have been dismissed after one year. I wish I recorded that.

Mr howard v. Neff III, executive director of the judicial conduct comittee, aiding and abetting, [BAR member], Ive written to this man 3 times,you should see the twisted responses from this man, from what his twisted words say: a judge can comitt as many felony crimes as they want, sure can !!! thats my understanding, and I wonder how many people are in jail for no reason, or how many people this judge has screwed, probably thousands, He is the executive director and said "he has no jurisdiction over legal descisions"? I wrote back saying there NEVER was any legal descision, because I never went to court. But there is numerous Misconducts of lawlessness, he just wrote back with more twisted words and denial, doesnt matter if the judge wrongfully steals property or wrongfully sentences somebody to 6 months or a year jail time, thats a legal descision ya see and he cant do anything about that. This is what makes it VERY DANGEROUS to show up in a "fake court" with a goddam psychopath sadist.

Abet

Definition

To criminally assist another person in the commission of a crime including in planning a crime, escaping from a crime, or in the actual commission of the crime.

Illustrative case law

See, e.g. Gonzales v. Duenas-Alvarez, 549 U.S. 183 (...

Sick people who smile or feel good, while they cause you hurt by thier cruel actions, theyll destroy your life, steal your property, lock you up, coerce you to sign a contract unwillingly, this is one FUCKIN SICK WOMAN, and her gang [clerks] theyre all very sick, They think they are God and are untouchable, they are satanic and very wicked, they have no empathy for another human [soul], This is 99% of them [judges clerks police] all doing it, thier paycheck means most to them too,

Sadistic personality disorder

Sadistic personality disorder is a personality disorder involving sadism which appeared in an appendix of the *Diagnostic and Statistical Manual of Mental Disorders* (DSM-III-R).[1] The later versions of the DSM (DSM-IV, DSM-IV-TR and DSM-5) do not include it.

Definition[edit]

Sadism involves deriving pleasure through others undergoing discomfort or pain. The opponent-process theory explains the way in which individuals not only display, but also enjoy committing sadistic acts.[2] [*clarification needed*] Individuals possessing sadistic personalities tend to display recurrent aggression and cruel behavior.[3][4] Sadism can also include the use of emotional cruelty, purposefully manipulating others through the use of fear, and a preoccupation with violence.[5]

Theodore Millon claimed there were four subtypes of sadism, which he termed *enforcing sadism*, *explosive sadism*, *spineless sadism*, and *tyrannical sadism*.[6][7][8][9][10]

Tyrannical sadism	Including negativistic features	Relishes menacing and brutalizing others, forcing them to cower and submit; verbally cutting and scathing, accusatory and destructive; intentionally surly, abusive, inhumane, unmerciful.

Procedural Due Process Civil

The Fifth Amendment says to the federal government that no one shall be "deprived of life, liberty or property without due process of law." The Fourteenth Amendment, ratified in 1868, uses the same eleven words, called the Due Process Clause, to describe a legal obligation of all states

SECTION 1. All persons born or naturalized in the United States, and subject to the jurisdiction thereof, are citizens of the United States and the State wherein they reside. No State shall make or enforce any law which shall abridge the privileges or immunities of citizens of the United States; nor shall any State deprive any person of life, liberty, or property, without due process of law; nor deny to any person within its jurisdiction the equal protection of the laws.

The Requirements of Due Process.—Although due process tolerates variances in procedure "appropriate to the nature of the case,"751 it is nonetheless possible to identify its core goals and requirements. First, "[p]rocedural due process rules are meant to protect persons not from the deprivation, but from the mistaken or unjustified deprivation of life, liberty, or property."752 Thus, the required elements of due process are those that "minimize substantively unfair or mistaken deprivations" by enabling persons to contest the basis upon which a state proposes to deprive them of protected interests.753 The core of these requirements is notice and a hearing before an impartial tribunal. Due process may also require an opportunity for confrontation and cross-examination, and for discovery; that a decision be made based on the record, and that a party be allowed to be represented by counsel.

Section 242 of Title 18 makes it a crime for a person acting under color of any law to willfully deprive a person of a right or privilege protected by the Constitution or laws of the United States.

For the purpose of Section 242, acts under "color of law" include acts not only done by federal, state, or local officials within the their lawful authority, but also acts done beyond the bounds of that official's lawful authority, if the acts are done while the official is purporting to or pretending to act in the performance of his/her official duties. Persons acting under color of law within the meaning of this statute include police officers, prisons guards and other law enforcement officials, as well as judges, care providers in public health facilities, and others who are acting as public officials. It is not necessary that the crime be motivated by animus toward the race, color, religion, sex, handicap, familial status or national origin of the victim.

The offense is punishable by a range of imprisonment up to a life term, or the death penalty, depending upon the circumstances of the crime, and the resulting injury, if any.

TITLE 18, U.S.C., SECTION 242

Whoever, under color of any law, statute, ordinance, regulation, or custom, willfully subjects any person in any State, Territory, Commonwealth, Possession, or District to the deprivation of any rights, privileges, or immunities secured or protected by the Constitution or laws of the United States, ... shall be fined under this title or imprisoned not more than one year, or both; and if bodily injury results from the acts committed in violation of this section or if such acts include the use, attempted use, or threatened use of a dangerous weapon, explosives, or fire, shall be fined under this title or imprisoned not more than ten years, or both; and if death results from the acts committed in violation of this section or if such acts include kidnaping or an attempt to kidnap, aggravated sexual abuse, or an attempt to commit aggravated sexual abuse, or an attempt to kill, shall be fined under this title, or imprisoned for any term of years or for life, or both, or may be sentenced to death. Yeah well its a shame theres no-one to enforce this law, U.S.C. Is united states code>Federal Law and they ignore it.

your courtroom flag, as you'll notice the flag outside of the building is different from the one inside

The flags displayed in State courts and courts of the United States have gold or yellow fringes. That is your warning that you are entering into a foreign enclave, the same as if you are stepping into a foreign embassy and you will be under the jurisdiction of that flag. The flag with the gold or yellow fringe **has no constitution, no laws, and no rules of court,** and is not recognized by any nation on the earth, and is foreign to you and the United States of America.

MILITARY FLAG WITH THE GOLD FRINGE

Martial Law Flag "Pursuant to 4 U.S.C. chapter 1, §§1, 2, & 3; Executive Order 10834, August 21, 1959; 24 F.R.6865; a military flag is a flag that resembles the regular flag of the United States, except that it has a Yellow Fringe border on three sides. The President of the United States designates this deviation from the regular flag, by Executive Order, and in his capacity as Commander-in-Chief of the military. The placing of a fringe on the national flag, the dimensions of the flag and the arrangement of the stars in the union are matters of detail not controlled by statute, but are within the discretion of the President as Commander in Chief of the Army and Navy."

34 Ops. Atty. Gen. 83.

President, Dwight David Eisenhower, by Executive Order No.10834, signed on August 21, 1959 and printed in the Federal Register at 24 F.R. 6865, pursuant to law, stated that: "A military flag is a flag that resembles the regular flag of the United States, except that it has a yellow fringe border on three sides."

A yellow fringe is not authorized on a Title: 4: U.S.A.: Codes: Chapter: 1: Sec.: 1&2 flag. It is a mutilation (Sec.:3).

Gold Tassel Admiralty

This Flag, with yellow fringe, represents No nation and No constitution.

THE LAW OF THE FLAG

The Law of the Flag, an International Law, which is recognized by every nation of the planet, is defined as:

"... a rule to the effect that a vessel is a part of the territory of the nation whose flag she flies. The term is used to designate the RIGHTS under which a ship owner, who sends his vessel into a foreign port, gives notice by his flag to all who enter into contracts with the ship master that he intends the Law of that Flag to regulate those contracts, and that they must either submit to its operation or not contract with him or his agent at all." Ref.: Ruhstrat v. People, 57 N.E. 41

By the doctrine of "four cornering" the flag establishes the law of the country that it represents. For example, the embassies of foreign countries, in Washington D.C., are "four cornered" by walls or fencing, creating an "enclave." Within the boundaries of the "enclave" of the foreign embassy, the flag of that foreign country establishes the jurisdiction and law of that foreign country, which will be enforced by the Law of the Flag and international treaty. If you enter an embassy, you will be subject to the laws of that country, just as if you board a ship flying a foreign flag, you will be subject to the laws of that flag, enforceable by the "master of the ship," (Captain), by the law of the flag.

When you enter a courtroom displaying a gold or yellow fringed flag, you have just entered into a foreign country, and you better have your passport with you, because you may not be coming back to the land of the free for a long time. The judge sitting under a gold or yellow fringe flag becomes the "captain" or "master" of that ship or enclave and he has absolute power to make the rules as he goes. The gold or yellow fringe flag is your warning that you are leaving your Constitutionally secured RIGHTS on the floor outside the door to that courtroom.

This is exactly why so many judges are appointed, and not elected by the people. The Federal judges are appointed by the President, the national military commander in chief. The State judges are appointed by the Governors, the state military commanders. The judges are appointed because the courts are military courts and civilians do not "elect" military officers.

Under martial law, you are presumed guilty until proven innocent.
The gold-fringed flag only stands inside military courts that sit in summary court martial proceedings against civilians and such courts are governed in part by local rules, but more especially by "The Manual of Courts Martial", U.S., 1994 Ed., at Art. 99, (c)(1)(b), pg. IV-34, PIN 030567-0000, U.S. Government Printing Office, Wash. D.C. The details of the crimes that civilians can commit, that are classed as 'Acts of War,' cover 125 pages in the Manual of Courts Martial.

Under Article IV, section 3, of the Constitution for the united States of America, no new State shall be formed or erected within the Jurisdiction of any other State. So -- Why have the judges of the State and Federal courts been allowed to erect foreign enclaves within our public courthouses under a foreign flag with the yellow fringe upon the soil of your state? *[Beats the hell outta me !!?? probably because the british BAR mafia took over this country !]*

We just thought you would like to know, so that the next time you see this yellow fringed flag you will know what you are looking at and what it really means. If you are in Spain and you see the National Flag of Spain, you would know that you are under the jurisdiction of Spain; and their laws govern you at this time. You are officially NOTICED when you see their flag. This is an admiralty law that says that all who see this flag understand they are governed by the laws of the country that this flag represents. You SHOULD understand that the gold or yellow fringed flag signifies the same thing. It is a notice to you that you are under the rules and regulations of the military force that is flying that flag.

Are you familiar with martial law?

Does your attorney understand what this flag means?

"It is an elementary rule of pleading, that a plea to the jurisdiction is a tacit (silent) admission that the court has a right to judge the case and is a waiver to all exception to the jurisdiction." (Girty v. Logan, 6 Bush KY, 8). Patriots are subjected to much ridicule when they object to [Admiralty flag] the flag that appears in every government office and courtroom in the land.

What Does The Gold-Fringed Flag Signify?

It is commonplace to see a gold-fringed United States flag standing in the present-day courtrooms. Is the gold

fringe there for decoration only, or does it signify a certain jurisdiction? Make no mistake about it -- the American People have been put on notice that the normal constitutional
functions of government have been suspended and that their Land has been placed under martial law. The information below is not by any means exhaustive, but will at least point the reader in the right direction to do additional research on his own.

Pursuant to the "Law of the Flag," a military flag does result in jurisdictional implications when flown (Ruhstrat v. People, 57 N.E. 41, 45, 185 Ill. 133, 49 LRA 181, 76 Am).

Under the powers designated by these statutes, the President may: seize property, organize and control the means of production, seize commodities, assign military forces abroad, institute martial law, seize and control all transportation and communications, regulate the operation of private enterprise, restrict travel, and, in a plethora of particular ways, control the lives of all American citizens.... (United States Senate Report 93-549, 19 November 1973).

I have stood on the backs of giants like John Stormer, Frederic Bastiat, Lysander Spooner, Charles Lindbergh Sr., Ezra Pound, Eustace Mullins, G Edward Griffin, Anna von Reitz, Kurtis Kallenbach and so many more. These men and women gave me the tools i needed to learn the truth of the system. Some of these people have passed. Others are still fighting the crime syndicate. I am proud to be a part of the great awakening and to have each and every one of you reading this standing beside me as we expose the corruption and call for truth and justice to prevail.

"In truth, paradigm shifts start from a long way off, slowly gather momentum over time by mechanisms perhaps poorly understood, until some critical mass is achieved at which time, now very suddenly, the new rules burst forth, and life is different....potentially, hope and faith are restored, vision has been made clear, and option available to us are seen as obvious even though, a short time ago, no options seemed available."

JUSTINIAN-DECEPTION: (HIDDEN-FOREIGN-TEXT-KNOWN-AS-DOG-LATIN) The Mother of all Deceptions: The Concept of Modern Day Slavery:

By: Romley Stewart. https://aplanetruth.info/2017/12/04/justinian-deception-the-mother-of-all-deceptions-the-concept-of-modern-day-slavery/ https://justiniandeception.wordpress.com/

https://www.youtube.com/watch?v=isx44nK-80Y

This Article is not legal advice in any way, it is a story in relation to research and findings that have been uncovered in relation to such research directed at the grammatical appearance and the grammatical standing of Government, (Or what could be foreign de-facto governments) Court and Banking Contracts and Charges. This article hopefully may alert some of you to the dangers of entering into contracts when you are not aware of the importance of the **grammatical appearance of the languages** employed within such contracting paper instruments. Is the "legal title" you hold "really" saying what you assumed it to say? The Latin meaning for Latin is: **Concealed, Hidden.** If Rome holds the legal titles of the countries of the world, than it alone is the debtor, but if Rome has the ability to confer the legal title to a third party debtor! Rome becomes the benefactor of all such countries. This knowledge to confer such legal title, being the debtor of the world, to the unsuspecting masses, is the key to their success, Rome transfers itself from the world debtor to the world creditor via an incredible grammatical deception that you are/were never meant to know. The Latin meaning for BABYLON (BABY-LON) is: Baby for long time. That's why the infantry of the Roman Empire (UNITED STATES MILITARY) are called infantry, they are the infants, the children that have not grown up and never likely to.

At the age of majority (21) when they are handed their Key to Life, such children are made sure that they are unaware of their true standing, and for that reason, such children remain holding the Rome military account (SURNAME) being the "cognomen" therefor remaining subject to the power of Rome and their true Christian Account (Ledger) is never claimed. After seven years, the child is legally presumed lost as sea and the Christian Credit Account remains under the control of Rome. The STATE has become Father of the Child and the Military have become the loyal DOGS that serve the State and that's why their ID tags are called. (DOG-TAGS), because of their military language: DOG-LATIN. What did the child lose? his right to direct the Dominion, it remained under the control of the State because the child never claimed it back at the age of Majority. The GOD of the Pagan (Pay-Again debtor of the Vatican) being the VATICAN, the world debtor, the legal title holder of Eden. The VATICAN is the: **Beast of Burden**, of man and by holding any accounts of Rome, you become the **servant of the Beast** by holding the **Mark of the Beast, being dogged: DOG-LATIN**. You have left the true God. You hold the dogged: DOG-LATIN text, and you are assumed: DEAD, chattels of the STATE, chattels of the VATICAN, you are the property of Rome.

Justice is a straight line, DOG-LATIN is the bending of the line, the corruption, the spurious document, the declension, the debasement, the counterfeit, the immoral act that no positive law could ever follow. It is the clever deception that "PEOPLE ASSUMED THIS TEXT WAS ENGLISH" and that's how you corrected the error in the name, it was never your name in the first place... This deception was right under your nose in plain sight all your life but because it was always there, you didn't notice it.

Usurper) G-O-D simply stands for "Grantor Of Dominion"... The grantor is the master, the grantee is the Slave-servant.

Anything rendered in the ALL UPPERCASE TEXT such as a name, or a town, or a street, or a suburb or an address or a State or even two or more capital letters joined together without a space renders a "presumption" it is not a fact! and this is where the "Presumption of Law" derives from. the ALL UPPER CASE SIGN language is not written text! it is a picture, an illustration, a symbol, it is the "JOKER" within the document. *Blacks Law Dictionary 4th Edition*. **An Account of "Grammatical Crimes" of Corporate Governance, courts and enforcement agencies by the use of DOG-LATIN: a "debased" criminal immoral foreign written language that renders all such DOG-LATIN documents, tendered by such corporate private governments, as "counterfeit". DOG-LATIN is unhyphenated all uppercase Latin symbolic text that follows the grammatical rules of English and not the grammatical rules of Latin. It is the language of the Illiterate, (*Blacks Law Dictionary 4th Edition*) it looks just like English, "IT LOOKS JUST LIKE THIS" but grammatically, it is the deception right under your nose... It is the poison in the text, it is the corruption in the contract. If you hold any part of this debased criminal all uppercase text of the dead corporations, such as your Driver License, you are claiming membership to the Underworld, criminal counterfeit, corrupt, corporate world of the Dead Corporations. You become a criminal.**

The "presumption" of a foreign military occupation of our country under the foreign control of Rome:

In 1973, Whitlam, Prime Minister of "AUSTRALIA" signed us up to a private military "Roman" contracting system of governance called: "UNIDROIT", head office in Rome. This is why the written language and its relationship to Private Contracts is so important to be aware of. The UNITED STATES, being the de-facto government of the **United States of America**, is now also a part of **UNIDRIOT**, under the power of Rome. DOG-LATIN (Debased Latin) appears to be the official language of the Infants: Military, infantry of Rome. It appears to be the language of the DEAD, (Debtor) and the only way you can hold a military name is in the ALL UPPERCASE APPEARANCE of the dead language: LATIN and or DOG-LATIN, being the designation of things and not proper names, such as your SURNAME. Proper Latin appears to be the official language of Rome and we **"Assume"** that DOG-LATIN (Debased Latin) is the language of the military debtor accounts/ledgers of Rome and a lack of understanding of such facts may be the cause of many Australians and people from around the world, to be losing their property and all their common law birth rights via a lack of understanding in relation to the appearance of such LATIN-TEXT-AND-ITS-DOGGED-CORRUPTION.

Anything rendered in the ALL UPPERCASE TEXT such as a name, or a town, or a street, or a suburb or an address or a State or even two or more capital letters joined together without a space renders a "presumption" it is not a fact! and this is where the "Presumption of Law" derives from. the ALL UPPER CASE SIGN language is not written text! it is a picture, an illustration, a symbol, it is the "JOKER" within the document. ***Blacks Law Dictionary 4th Edition***.

as part of law by Acts Va. 1785, c. 65 (1 Hening's St. at Large, p. 162), Rev. Code 1819, c. 107, and Code 1849, c. 110 (Code 1930, § 5117 et seq.). Jacobs v. Jacobs, 100 W. Va. 585, 131 S.E. 449, 453.

JOKER. In political usage, a clause in legislation that is ambiguous or apparently immaterial, inserted to render it inoperative or uncertain without arousing opposition at the time of passage. Bennet v. Commercial Advertiser Ass'n, 230 N.Y. 125, 129 N.E. 343, 344.

JOLT. A sudden shock or jerk; a jolting motion, as in a vehicle moving over a rough street —

A lot of needed information is here for individual people. Posted on November 12, 2014 by arnierosner On Nov 12, 2014, at 11:05 AM,
http://www.annavonreitz.com/

Anna von Reitz wrote: The key word to pay attention to is "person"—- Congress specifically redefined the word "person" in 1862 to mean "corporation"——so that is what "person" means throughout federal code (as in secret code) unless specifically and explicitly defined in another way within an individual document or piece of legislation. You will also be interested to know that in subsequent action, Congress claimed to OWN all federal corporations and their assets. So if you admit to being a "person" you are letting them slide by and claim to own you and your assets, literally. They have used and abused your property— your given name which was clearly given to you by your parents as your intellectual property — to create and name incorporated entities after you, and then used these legal fiction entities —- foreign situs trusts, ESTATES, transmitting utilities—- as a means to bring false charges against you in foreign jurisdictions and then also to establish liens against these legal fiction entities that they then use to defraud your actual estate. Note— living people don't have names. They have appellations. Only "things" have names. Living people don't have signatures, either. They have autographs. American State Citizens don't have "civil rights" they have "Natural and Unalienable Rights". You have been taught to "sign" your "name" since you were in grade school, yet I have just told you that you don't have a name—- you have an appellation that you are "called by" and you don't have a signature, either—-only an autograph. What is going on here? A fraud scheme so vast as to be unimaginable. Why have you been taught to "sign" "your name"? And to do it in a precise and specific way—- Upper and Lower Case, First-Middle-Last??? Because all "persons" using Names in the form: "John Quincy Adams" were "defined" as foreign situs trusts belonging to the "federal franchise States" such as the "State of Ohio" as property. You were summarily defined as chattel belonging to the federal corporation and its franchises, standing as collateral for all the debts of the United States of America, Incorporated, — a privately owned and operated commercial corporation—-and its "State" franchises, operated just like local franchises of Burger King. You were tricked into giving false evidence against yourself every time you "signed" any piece of paper, every time you admitted to having a "name", and you were deliberately taught this by a public school system run by the perpetrators of this FRAUD. So what has happened since then? Why, they've spun off new legal fiction entities and named them all after you. The debts of the United States of America, Inc. and all its franchises including old "John Quincy Adams" — were finally discharged in bankruptcy as of July 1, 2013. Now they have to sell you o new masters and retrain you to use a "signature" with only a middle initial —- another "name" in a slightly different form: "John Q. Adams". These entities are all transmitting utilities owned and operated by the UNITED NATIONS CORPORATION doing business as the (new) FEDERAL RESERVE doing business as "states" named simply "OHIO" or "ALASKA" or "MONTANA". Are you a transmitting utility? Hmm? Did you knowingly, willingly, and under conditions of full disclosure agree to stand as surety for any privately owned commercial corporation doing business as the United States of America, Inc.? Did you ever agree to becoming a "United States Citizen" and giving your earthly estate to a privately owned and operated French commercial corporation doing business as the UNITED STATES? No? Did you agree to having all your assets (including your body) rolled over into a Puerto Rican ESTATE trust administered under the laws and in the foreign jurisdiction of the United States of America (Minor)—— a deceptively named "union" of "American" "states" that most of us think of as "federal territories and possessions"? Well, if not, then, it is high time that you objected to all this fraud and false claims being made against you and your property interests by the members of "Congress" who are not acting as your deputies—men and women obligated to act as your fiduciaries —but are instead pretending to be merely your "representatives" —— free to "represent" you as anything and anyone that they like—including a "person", to indebt you as they please, and to subject you to their whims and the whims of their creditors. It's time. Take back your standing as a living, breathing, vital American State Citizen—- a being endowed with more civil authority on the land in your little finger than the entire "federal government". Realize how you have been misled, defrauded, enslaved, and disserved. And realize that this was all brought to you by men you trusted and respected — people like Franklin Delano Roosevelt and Winston Churchill— who excused their profound criminality as being "necessary for the war effort" and their successors (except for John Fitzgerald Kennedy) who continued the abuse under the pretense that they were in a constant "state of war" and that this somehow justified their actions and granted them authority to enslave you and trump up debt against you and your private property. It's THEIR war. Let THEIR "citizens" fund and fight it. Remember always that President Andrew Johnson declared three times on the public record that the American states were at peace after the Civil War—- the civil government and the peaceful inhabitants of the land of The United States of America (Major) have been at peace for 150 years. As an American State Citizen born on the land of the _____State (for example, Ohio State, not the State of Ohio which is a federal "state") you are inhabiting the land jurisdiction and have every right to stand firmly upon it. Their occupying army is utterly obligated to protect you and your property and to return it all to you unharmed, or they will all be recognized as war criminals by the rest of the world and held to account for it. Their charters will be cancelled, all their corporations liquidated, and their assets returned to their creditors—- you. This is the way it stands and the way it really is. Now that you know, you are responsible for re-educating yourself and others. And you are responsible for knowing that you are NOT a "person" nor a "thing", but a living breathing and fully mentally competent American State Citizen.

case monetization,

CRIS court registry investment systems= monetizing court cases for big money$$$, look on the first one online is a 66 page report showing numbers in the millions and hundreds of millions of $ $$ and check the other links for more information, these are very slimey criminals !!!!!. Although nobody has yet found a report on a traffic court,,,,,,,this is all we need to see for now to establish an articulable reason to believe what they are doing, and they protect their accounting like the holy graile, so im surprised to find this information below. I can remember data processors coming into the jail working 3rd shift all night on the computers. They looked indian. You could see them through the glass all night long sitting at the computers and left at 7AM in the morning,

I asked the correctional officer and she told me they were data processors. AH HA, yeah. I would think it takes professional skills to do this as most clerks are not trained book-keepers or accountants, also a knowledge of financial securities needed. I was sleeping in the suicide ward out on the floor and watched them during the night. [Yeah some frikkin whacko doctor baker acted me, guess that pays more for them]. I always wondered how they can transfer all the funds, transfer securities, & and disperse all their payments to the departments of the performance contract[s]. makes sence to do this kind of work at the jail all night because the courthouse is busy all day and locked up at night with all their security systems. [just my speculation for now]

PDF]

Case Monetization (CRIS Report) - AntiCorruption Society

https://anticorruptionsociety.files.wordpress.com › 2011/01 › case-monetiz...

1.

DISTRICT **CASE** NUMBER. D04SCX
2185-CV-1049. D05TXE 1 :00-CV-621.
D05TXE 1 :00-CV-621. D05TXE 1 :00-
CV-819. D05TXE 1 :00-CV-819.
D05TXE ...

Monetising the IoT: Finding the Right Monetisation Model - IoT ...

Court Registry Investment System (CRIS) | Middle District of ...

https://www.ncmd.uscourts.gov › court-registry-investment-system-cris

1.

The Court Registry Investment System
(CRIS) is an interest-bearing cash ...

mature each week to pay out funds for
all registry **cases** settled during the
week.

Missing: ~~monetization~~ | Must include: **monetization**

Improving Court Case Management, Financial Systems, and ...

https://www.uscourts.gov › statistics-reports › improving-court-case-manag...

1.

Design the Next Generation of
Electronic **Case** Management System
for ... of court financial managers and
the AO are developing the next
generation **CRIS**, ...

Case Monetizing and The Selling Of Your Rights! - Alibertatum

https://therightsofthefew.com › case-monetizing-and-the-selling-of-your-ri...

1.

Apr 25, 2018 - Did you know that every
time there is a **case** of any kind that a
negotiable instrument created. ... **case-
monetization-cris_report**-07-2003-
b.pdf ...

Information for learning:

The United States is a Corporation   http://freedom-school.com/the-united-states-is-a-corporation.html

Yes, you read the title correctly. We are not living in a country with a government of the people, by the people, for the people, but we are part of a giant Corporation, The United States Corporation, and the President of America is the CEO. We are only the employees. This Corporation, in its turn, is owned by another Corporation, The British Crown.

"Hey, wait a minute! First of all, America is not owned by Great Britain," you may way. "That's what the War of Independence was all about; to free ourselves from British tyranny. We are free from Britain and we have our own Constitution. Our Founding Fathers helped out with that!"

If this is what you think, it is incorrect, and I will tell you why. We have never been free from Britain; the power only changed from overt power to covert power. They gave us an illusion of freedom, and they have succeeded well to keep their little secret. Thus, the Founding Fathers, who most of them were Freemasons, had no intention to give us any freedom. They worked hand in glove with the British Crown all the time, but the only way to establish a "New World" in America was to fool the people and tell them that they were fighting for freedom. This is the plain truth in a nutshell, but now it's time to back up and explain the above a little deeper...

Corporation of the People, by the People, for the People

(The following section is an excerpt from David Icke's book, The David Icke Guide to the Global Conspiracy [and how to end it] pp. 231-233. I strongly recommend this book, because it gives you a brilliant overview of how this conspiracy works. You can order the book at www.davidicke.com)

The United States 'government' is actually the United States Corporation. It was created behind the screen of a 'Federal Government' when, after the manufactured 'victory' in the American War on 'Independence', the British colonies exchanged overt dictatorship from London for the far more effective covert dictatorship that has been in place ever since.

In effect, the Virginia Company, the corporation headed by the British Crown that controlled the 'former' colonies, simply changed its name to the United States of America and other related pseudonyms. These include the US, USA, United States of America, Washington DC, District of Columbia (Samurais) and the President of the Corporation is known as the President of the United States. This is an accurate title given that one is the names for the Corporation is the 'United States'. He or she is not the President of the people or the country as they are led to believe - that's just the smokescreen.

This means that Bush launched a 'war on terrorism' on behalf of a private Corporation to further the goals of that Corporation. It had nothing to do with 'America' or 'Americans', because these are very different legal entities. It is the United States Corporation, not the 'government', which owns the United States military and everything else that comes under the term 'federal'. The privately-owned Corporation called the United States is the holding company, if you like, and the fifty states are its subsidiaries.

You may have noticed that the national flag of the United States always has a gold fringe when displayed in court or federal buildings, and you see this also in federally-funded schools and on the uniforms of US troops. Under the International Law of the Flags, a gold fringe indicates the jurisdiction of commercial law, also known as British Maritime Law, and, in the US, as the Uniform Commercial Code, or UCC. The gold fringe is not part of the American flag known as the Stars and Stripes, but it is a legal symbol indicating that the court, government building, school or soldier is operating under British Maritime Law and the Uniform Commercial Code; military and merchant law.

For example, if you appear in a court with a gold-fringed flag your constitutional rights are suspended, and you are being tried under British Maritime (military/merchant) Law. If it seems strange that a court or building on dry land could be administered under Maritime or Admiralty Law, look at US Code, Title 18 B 7. It says that Admiralty Jurisdiction is applicable in the following locations:

1) the high seas
2) any American ship
3) any lands reserved or acquired for the use of the United States, and under the exclusive or concurrent jurisdiction thereof, or any place purchased or otherwise acquired by the United States by consent of the legislature of the state. In other words, mainland America.

All this is founded on Roman law, which goes back to Babylon and Sumerian law; because the Illuminati have been playing this same game throughout the centuries wherever they have gone. The major politicians know that this is how things are and so do the top government administrators, judges, lawyers and insider 'journalists'.

Americans think that their government and legal system is pegged in some way to the Constitution, but it is not. The United States, like Britain and elsewhere, is ruled by commercial law to overcome the checks and balances of common law. It's another monumental fraud. The US court system does not operate under the American Constitution, but under corporate law. It is the law of contracts and you have to make a contract with the Corporation for that law to legally apply to you.

The scam has been set up so that when you register with the 'Federal Government' in any way, by accepting a Social Security Number, driver's license, or any of the other official federal documents, you are, unknowingly, contracting to become an asset-employee of the United States Corporation...Every word, or use of lower/upper case, is making a legal statement. Have you noticed that when you receive correspondence relating to government, law and anything to do with finance, including taxation, your name is always spelt in all upper case, as in BILL JONES?

But your upper case name is not you. It is a corporation/trust set up by the 'government' Corporation through the treasury department at your birth. Every time a child is born a corporation/trust is created using his or her name in all upper case. So BILL JONES is what they call a 'straw man', a corporate, not human, entity. They do it this way because governments are corporations and they operate under commercial law, the law of contracts. The laws passed by governments only apply to corporations and not to living, breathing, flesh and blood, sovereign, free men and women spelt in upper and lower case, or all lower case, as with Bill Jones, or bill jones. The living, breathing sovereign man and woman is subject to common law, not eh commercial law introduced by governments through legislation.

Using commercial law makes it much easier to install an 'elected' dictatorship. Unlike common law, you are not subject to precedents built up over centuries. You simply have to get a majority to vote for a bill in Parliament of Congress, or have the US President sign a document, and the law is imposed. What you also have to do - clearly not difficult - is to keep from the people the knowledge that their name in all upper case is not them. They will then pay you taxes and be subject to your jurisdiction and control in all areas of their lives, by unknowingly standing surety for the corporation - 'BILL JONES' - that they don't even know exists.

All court documents have the person's name in all upper case because under the law of contracts the living, breathing being cannot be tried under corporate law, only a corporate entity can. It is so crazy that Americans pay personal income tax to the government (corporation) via the Internal Revenue Service (IRS) when the law to introduce personal income tax was never passed. Ask anyone from the US government or IRS to produce the law that says Americans must pay income tax on their wages and they will not be able to do it. Many have tried and the law has never been revealed because it doesn't exist...A $50,000 reward was offered by the We The People organization to anyone who could produce the law and IRS agent, Sherry Jackson, thought it would be easy money. She then found out that there was no law and resigned to become a campaigner against this fantastic hoax...

...Yet, when people don't pay taxes, which they do not legally have to pay, the IRS takes their property, puts them in jail, and ever more often sends in the armed goons in the black masks. It's fascism, nothing less...If anyone thinks that without personal income tax there would be no education and other public services - it's not true. They are paid for by state and property taxes, business taxes, sales taxes, fuel tax, booze tax and all the other endless taxation that we pay besides income tax. In fact, personal income tax in the US is roughly the same as the money paid by government to the banks in interest on loans.

United States as a Corporation:

See HERE

Also, see HERE

An etymology of the word "corporation." HERE

HERE

(15) "United States" means—
(A) a Federal corporation;

(B) an agency, department, commission, board, or other entity of the United States; or

(C) an instrumentality of the United States.

Queen Elizabeth controls and has amended U.S. Social Security www.opsi.gov.uk/si/si1997/1997

With no constitutional authority to do so, Congress creates a separate form of government for the District of Columbia, a ten mile square parcel of land (see, Acts of the Forty-first Congress," Section 34, Session III, chapters 61 and 62). Act 1871 allows the "Corp US" to control the country in the place of the natural Government HERE and HERE

Some information I found how the courts operate.

I would try some of these methods but they do not respond to anything, they want to lock me up until they get what they want $$

'Golden Key'

"Innocent is the antonym of the stars: Culprits they are."

"What is it to ask that of a Kings ransom compared to the bounty of the universe? One says give One the Heavens! What is the answer to the question? Wisdom, Let us look into the paths of the stars and see what is their design, and what melodies they have sung, and they shall sing, as it is their gravity that leads us, as gravity = time, so is One born in the salty by product of alchemy: as the Sea is an accumulation of all the tears throughout the ages over the struggle by the Gods to manipulate the soul"...srqu.

IT is the ISSUE.
What is IT? It is the issue of interest to proceeds. Either way it does not matter whether it is in court or out, past or present issue or even what the issue is over.

It is the assessment, **It** is what must be ascertained to discover what **It** is. Where does one find **It**?? This depends upon the 'theatre'. Example: if one has an 'alleged' issue cognizable by a court then there must be registered with the court the 'assessment' to discover **It** one must do a search with the head of the theatre, I. E. the clerk of the court to ascertain what claims have been registered in the court in the name of THE OFFENDER.

1. Ask the head clerk for a certified copy of all judgments registered with the court in the name of THE OFFENDER.
2. If none exist, then there is no assessment.
3. Without an assessment there can be no demand for performance
4. Without a demand for performance, there can be no neglect
5. Without neglect there can be no crime
6. Without a crime there can be no court proceeding

When you get to the point of them addressing you, you ask for the attorney/ prosecutor, CFO to read the charges on to the record or properly **"Declare the issue"** (as you cannot SEE them as of yet) [read the Kobe Bryant case] when This is done, it puts the burden of proof upon them [calls them out, margin call]. Until that is done it is all presumption, and that is what they want you to argue about 'presumption' or "non-issue'. Or "speculation." **They are trying to avoid the issue. Issue being the issuance of the bond.**

The industrial society pays the interest to you when they release the order of the court (calling the bailee to the floor), **to put the deficiency on the docket**, and instructing the deputy of the circuit court to call the calendar, Bottom line, interest accrues from the principal and for the account to close, the interest must return to the principal. All taxes are interest payments back to the original owner principal).

What is it? It is the issue. They are making an issue by making the claim, the claim being proceeds, hat is the issue, the proceeds. Claim=proceeds. Proceeds=issue. Issue =claim Where is the issue and what are the proceeds. They are coming forward claiming there is an issue, but they are trying to avoid declaring the issue at the same time.

This is the **"Why"** Without the why is to be without power. [Merovingian/ The Matrix]

This is Public vs. Private.

These are "Public offerings" they are dealing in. But they are trying to get you to agree to keep them 'Private" by not "declaring the issue" and getting you to argue [identifying the issue for them] over a 'non-issue" therefore avoiding the registration of the bond. This is laid out clearly in title 26 sec. 6049 and 4701. Private bonds are NOT required to be registered. That is why using the "Bills of exchange" are so dangerous. They can use those in any way they like to further fund their extortion. It is like cash to them [drug money, like fed notes] although it is coming from you, the "True Creator" it is still a derivative, not the real thing because it is "speculation" and so none of it is a reality until the "issue is declared." When they are compelled to "Declare the issue" that now "charges" the circuit and brings the "Issue" to light, that can now be Discharged. This is creation in reality.

Think of the Mirror the reflection has to come from the substance.
The Reflection cannot make the Substance Appear only the Substance can command the Reflection.
They are approaching us with the "proposed" reflection and asking us to become the substance to make the reflection appear.....only one problem the reflection does not command the substance.
There 'evidence' is the "proposed" reflection.....the reflection is the product (and fixture 1099 oid) of the substance not vice-versa. Can you "see" why they want the uninformed people of the world out there advising' people to do an 'acceptance' of their erroneous public offer and include a 'private' bill of exchange???

1. **Burden of Proof is waived by 'acceptor'**
2. **Unregistered (illicit) public offer is converted to 'private' bond (not required to be registered title 26 6049)**
3. **Private bonds have value; illicit Public Offers are a 'liability' (supported by statutory policy)**
4. **Doesn't get much sweeter; and "people" feel "good" about funding this form of terrorism......**
5. **Notice how when you give the BOE's to them they disappear never to be seen again and they are still disputing over the alleged issue?**

Ok, here is a ship docked in a port. Now there are these pirates offloading the products[cargo] off the back of the ship and paying off customs and the captain and taking the products over to the beach and selling it bootleg for black market script [fed notes] and of course stealing "private offerings" [BOE's and the like from those whom are foolish enough to believe they are going to be "registered"]... instead of the product being taken off the ship and declared thru the "Public" like it is supposed to be. Your signature is the only thing of value. You create the issues, the issues generate the interest, the interest returns to the principal, you, [money of Account vs. money of Exchange] Don't believe me, ok, everybody stop , don't sign anything for one day!!!! If nobody signed anything for one day, the system would crash!!!, now you need to learn to use it to your own prosperity. You CANNOT "discharge" the "charge" in any other kind without engaging in piracy. There is no government outside the corporation other than oligarchy. Since the entire system of commerce has been perverted and "we the people" are now without Power [the why]. Do you think they do not know this and have not plotted, manipulated and nurtured it to perfection of chaos, "piracy at its Finest."

1.**"Please properly declare the alleged issues for the record,"**
2. **I want to postpone any pleadings until I get the bill of particulars.**
3. **If there is an issue with the involvement of an identity in the resemblance of my ordinate appellation, then as the principal I have an interest in the "Bill of particulars" of the proceeds, products, accounts, fixtures and services."**

One prays for the disclosure of the first ledger entry allowing for the double booking journal.

Be careful as they will try to play a little bait and switch and the judge will try to get away with reading the charges for the prosecutor. They are still NOT VISIBLE until the accuser /attorney or prosecutor "**reads them into the record." [Declares the issue]** any and all previous presentments have been erroneous "speculation" to this point.

Failure on their part to have this done is **"denial of due process"** and can bring the case back no matter how much water flows under the bridge.

Now tell the judge you would like to **postpone your pleadings** until you get **the bill of particulars**. This would be in proper "form" with OMB numbers. This I believe is the actual "call" when you ask them to "Declare the issue."

Ascertaining the "proceeds" of a tax exempt bond "issue" is generally the first step needed to be undertaken to ensure compliance in the burden of proof [with arbitrage restrictions]. "proceeds, products, accounts, fixtures and services."

Ask for the CUSIP #. of any and all bonds **[Commission on Uniform Securities Identification Process numbers. These ARE the issues!]**, YOUR copy of the 1099OID filings, the complete audit trail, vouchers, backend copies, omad, and omid. Name of the damaged party, name of the issuer, who is the real party of interest, who is the holder of the account, who signed the forms generating the bonds as Attorney in fact! Copy of your Authorization for all transactions.

R: 2003] : it might be time to direct attention to those who have the means to develop the methods one can issue or purchase options to SHORT actions that are taken like is against me, whereby the jail or warehouse holding the collateral can be put in the option to deliver the stock (prisoner) in the event of a margin call.

Stockbroker might know people who are capable of working out these details even he isn't. Remember –the options are to be charged to the time it takes for the stock item to reach –0– bankruptcy. That condition might be determined in the equity statement or margin call when the bankruptcy is discovered. That might be when they miss their margin call etc. In these cases, they cannot use borrowed funds so the particular account will have to carry all the funds used to operate until maturity. This is where options come into play. Their purchase order is chargeable to the principal in the account and the option purchased is opposed to the victim who requests release to him. Then he needs to go <u>short</u> as well with his options too. Now it is evident that the principal and victim are the same, then the discovery of the insolvent adversary leaves the victim in possession of the principal and the other just had his option run out.

I strongly suspect when a warrantless arrest occurs, like they did to me, the same outfit that did this also sold options to pay their way up front. Those are the options that take the principal charge to –0-. They are averaged in reverse. These are what shows the bankruptcy and when they go SHORT they are also FORTH (or Fourth) which means that some sort of a tax deferral exists in each quarter of the taxable year and the forth quarter is the quarter which sums up the tax deferrals etc. The end of the fiscal year. The end of the fiscal year in my case would be 90 days after I was arrested!

When we follow the process outlined above, we do not need a broker to do the "Call". We can accomplish it ourselves right there in the court room.

The three elements of a contract:

1. Offer: **The Burdon of proof lies squarely on the shoulders of the "declarant of an issue"**

2. Acceptance. *Meeting of the minds*: **If a claim has been made and no issue has been declared, there is no issue of record other than the "default" which IS now the only issue of record.**

3. Consideration: **The Sovereign may now redeem the assessment of the issue.**

Where is the superior pre–existing contract?
Who is the real party of interest?
Where is the damaged property and the verified assessment of its value?

Let us get to the crux of the situation. We have "we the people of America" and the US Government Corporation. If "we the people" contract to become members of the US Corporation, there is no longer "we the people of America" as the Dejure Government, [organized sovereign body] as the Constitution says "by the people, for the people, of the people." It is now the US government Corporation elect. Since all the US citizens through contract have signed away the sovereignty of the "we the people." They now have become "Members" of the "Corporation." But wait now, they have also signed a treaty with us, "The Constitution" which article 1 sec 10 clause 1, is the crux. " Congress shall make no laws impairing the obligations of contract". So what is our first element of a contract? Yes, meeting of the minds, FULL DISCLOSURE. Period, with out this, there is NO contract. But here we have a treaty offered, made a public offering, but you have not "ACCEPTED" them on public record.

This is the Superior pre existing contract [treaty] between them and us. You must compel performance by your servants.

Establishing the "Record."

No matter who or what the situation it is you must get their oaths on record, especially in court cases.
The judge,
the clerk
the prosecutor,
the district attorney, or county attorney
your attorney
and of course his contract between you and him whether he is court appointed or you are paying him, put a "CERTIFIED COPY" "APOSTILLED!!!!" of their OATH on the COURT RECORD "Accepted" , sign it and have it notarized and be sure to get copies and send everyone a copy of their accepted oaths and the contracts of the attorneys, and your court appointed attorney!

This is the ONLY signed verified affidavit that you ever get from them. This is the only valid presentment ever provided. It is IMPERATIVE to have it in a binding contract to compel performance! Everything else are ALL erroneous presentments.

By placing the accepted oath and fidelity bond on the "record" that Bonds the case, then using the apostille gives it "Judicial notice" which is now the only "declared issue" of record. This moves their fidelity bond to the credit side of the account..

The Constitution is not something that gives you rights, you have liberty to not be beleaguered or molested by the corp of US. The Constitution is and their oath to it are a parameter they solemnly swore to stand within. You are only Directing them to do two things, to stand within their parameters of their solemnly sworn oath and to perform the duties to provide the proceeds, products, accounts, fixtures and services. "declare the issues" and provide the bill of particulars.

You must supersede the public defenders/opposing attorney's contract with the court by writing up an acceptance letter for his assistance to you and putting it on the court record showing he works for you!! **Make a new contract between you and him, thanking him for him working for you and having your best interest at heart. The court cannot expect any benefits from the gifting of the assistance of the court appointed attorney either. Now you can ask for the consideration. Declaration of the issues postponement of any pleadings and the bill of particulars.**

It IS ALL about the contracts, that is what the courts are there DOING! Enforcing contracts. You put the contracts on the court record and the acceptance of contracts to there oaths and they will stand on their own.

In the case of credit collection, If you have paid service charges for anything that is a contract that you can formally accept. Now there is a contract in place showing the CFO works for you and you can compel performance. [complete audit trail]

Even CPA's have an oath to IRS saying they will follow the rules, IRS form f23 that is an acceptable contract. CONTRACT IS KING!

Check out Treasury dept circular No. 230 (Rev 6-2005) also see the Sarbane-Oxley Act.

The Superior Contract is the Oath of Office, you see any one accepting a public office had to agree to protect the Public in order to gain a position.... As it is not the public's intent to harm itself by empowering someone ABOVE it .... It was simply to provide a SERVANT within certain parameters to serve it.   That is the Contract.   But what happens when an essential element to contract is missing:????

The three elements of a contract:

4. Offer
5. Acceptance. Meeting of the minds
6. Consideration.

Offer: The Oath of Office
Acceptance: Have we accepted the "public offer"???? (Not yet but we can and will fix that)
Consideration: "Public servants" standing within the parameters of their solemn sworn oath and performing the duties of providing the proceeds products accounts fixtures and services

You know the old saying ' the show must go on' well that is exactly what is going on. The Public Actors are putting on a show; the people were supposed to be the "directors" but failed to fulfill that "role" by executing an acceptance of their "actor/ servants" Oath of Office and have instead have "elected" to become actors themselves. ("all the world is a stage !!!")

The Oath of Office is the "script" that must be followed on stage (in public) but if no "director" steps forward to bind the actor to the "script"; then, we get "Improvisation"!!!!!   That is why it is essential to form a binding agreement so that the stage will be defined and the script dictated by the directors (people) instead of the actors (public officials)

Get a Certified Copy of the Oath of Office
Do an Acceptance of the Oath of Office
Form a binding Contract with your servants!!
This is the link to the foia offices of the US Corp. for getting the oaths of the Servants.
 http://www.usdoj.gov/oip/foia_updates/Vol_XX_1/page3.htm

free information below found from a very experienced researcher,
One should be very leery of Paytriots for profit, who are selling so-called redemption packages and snake oil; especially, if they use the term STRAWMAN. They some how confuse or intermingle redemption, presentment and strawman. The Babylonian method of redemption involves the preparation of three documents (bonds) and one letter. The knowing how to prepare these and where to record these is the key. The Black Robed Devils have no mercy and will not allow room for any mistakes. Presentment is the action taken against public officials, who damage you; and can ONLY be accomplished, if so-called redemption has been perfected. In essence, the so-called redemption and presentment are similar, since these both involve bid bond, surety bond and performance bond, but for the most part are not referenced as bonds. However, court processes also involve these same three bond processes. Remember this, in Babylon, first in time WINS.

An officer issues a citation or complaint, the bid bond. They then come looking for your corporate fiction, your shadow. They find you and take you captive (like the winged monkeys took Dorothy), since they consider you to be the fiduciary for the mindless fiction or strawman (a felon, guilty before proven innocent). They drag you before some administrative magistrate, who converts you into the surety by conning you into posting bond, a booty that he and the officers receive a portion, thereof. Which then, makes you liable for whatever performance bond is determined by the Black Robed Devil some time in the future. They steal both your wealth and your time. Accepting RE-presentation, Appearing (Except by SPECIAL PRESENCE), stating ones name on or for the Record, or entering PLEA are sure losers. Each of these grants jurisdiction. Never state ones 'Nom de guerre' or name, NEVER! NEVER! A case must be won prior to or at Arraignment.

There are two things, which these DEVILS cannot do to their victims; they cannot arraign or sentence anyone, who is without RE-presentation. PERIOD. RE-present means to present as something other than as self. Once one enters, the sharks, lions and vipers are sure to pounce on their victim. Basically, it works this way the Black Robed Devil send the Gestapo out to pickup the "Trust", "Vessel" {49 USC §§ 1176-1282 Addendum}, Transmitting Utility {UCC 10-104} or so-called "Strawman" or "TIN man". The Gestapo finds you at the appointed address, you identity or accuse self and the Gestapo seizes you as the Fiduciary. They then take you, the assumed Fiduciary, before the administrative magistrate, who CONS or coerces you into becoming the Surety. Does recording of the Commercial Paper discussed in previous paragraphs begin to make sense? He, who files first, WINS! "...(A)n attorney [THE COURT'S JESTER] occupies a dual position which imposes dual obligations." His first duty is to the courts [THE BLACK ROBED DEVIL WHO IS GOING TO PUT YOU AWAY or EXTORT FROM YOU AS MUCH AS HE CAN POSSIBLY TAKE.] and the public [THE STATE], not the client [A FOOL'S FOOL], and wherever the duties to his client conflict with those he owes as an officer of the court in the administration of justice, the former must yield to the latter." - 7 CJS § 4. "Clients are also called 'wards of the courts' in regard to their relationship with their attorneys." - 7 CJS § 2. "Wards of court. Infants and persons of unsound mind." Which one are you? "Davis' Committee v. Loney, 290 Ky. 644, 162 S.W. 2d 189, 190." - Black's Law Dictionary, 6th Ed. ALL ATTORNEYS AND JUDGES HAVE AN ATTORNEY ON RETAINER TO REPRESENT THEM; THEREFORE THEY ARE ALL PERSONS OF UNSOUND MINDS. THIS IS MADNESS, BUT IT IS THEIR LAW.

Topic: The Uniform Securitization Scheme (the Birth Scam) *free information from the author sho says he wants to share it,*

https://archive.org/details/UniformSecuritizationSchemeBirthScam1

The universal boilerplate securities transaction blueprint that governs your commercial life.

ABSTRACT. Long form, short form, birth pledge, estate, cestui que trust, birth bond, BC bond. Treasury account, SSN, SS bond, DTC...This article explains the series of transactions that comprise the birth scam whereby governments convert the birth of a child into a financial asset to underwrite the public debt and the issuance of substance-shy currency. Dubbed by the author the Uniform Securitization Scheme or USS, this universal pattern of "legalization," registration, certification, securitization and general deposit is revealed to be a blueprint for virtually every event of our lives involving government, from simple purchases to the most complex banking, economic and Court transactions, in particular the metamorphosis of loan applications into salable securities. The article suggests that a comprehensive understanding of the birth schematic will provide the reader with a new plateau to address the complications when constitutors of the government face enticements to become its subjects. The author states that the article is offered to elevate discussion to a new plateau and assist concerned people in explaining their positions to friends and relatives. THE UNIFORM SECURITIZATION SCHEME INTRODUCTION. There was a time when the joyous event of childbirth was recorded in the family Bible to signify the child's status as a member of the family's posterity with implied rights of an heir. To this day, the family Bible remains a lawful record that is recognized in the "legal" system. In 1933, when most privately-held gold was confiscated by the Federal Reserve System under Executive Order 6102 and obligations payable in gold were outlawed under H.J.R. 192 (Public Law 73-10), the substance-backed economy was replaced by a financial system based upon credit (lOU's) which is currently failing under the weight of it's own nature. What is that nature? Like "Seinfeld," very simply, nothing. Empty promises to pay backed by fraudulent presumptions of informed consent. It's an economy where the books always add up to zero, where the very nature of bookkeeping had to be altered to disguise the void (double-entry bookkeeping), where the notion of a single entry to explain your purchase of a pack of gum was apparently inadequate to hide the theft of your money, where every asset is also entered as an offsetting liability, where the law itself had to be replaced by commercial hypocrisy, where the sum total of all activity in every government licensed institution, bank. Court and corporation equals zero each and every day, where transactions which once involved the exchange of goods and services of equal value now involve the exchange of "securities" of equal "value" (nothing) as the term "value" is defined in inferior statutory "law." Like "Seinfeld," the world suffers not so much an economy, as a comedy of errors. Perhaps more correctly, a comedy of frauds wherein the concept of "value" is established by words on the page instead of the perceived value of goods, services and labor at hand; where up is down, black is white, and timeless immorality is perfectly "legal." It is a well established fact that the United States is defined as a corporation in Section 3002 of the Judiciary Code. Meaning that the United States judiciary operates under the global presumption that the United States is a corporation, notwithstanding periodic attempts by learned attorneys-at-law to treat this fact casually. What is a corporation? In essence: nothing. A construction of words on pieces of paper. A contrivance without a soul, sentience or conscience. The question becomes, How does an unconscious paper corporation operating in an economy without substance control the population of living people under the original public trust charter? The answer is self-evident. Organized commercial fraud which applies ancient edifices of commercial sleight-of-hand such as legal fictions, certification, registration and securitization to achieve outcomes which would otherwise be impossible (and certainly repugnant to the Founders). Translation; the machines harness the people's commercial energy through a Matrix of scripted distractions and diversions wherein fraud, falsehood and fallacy supplant the law until amnesia has become endemic. That system is known as the "legal" system, a profit-inspired veneer for THE universal system of voodoo accounting explained in this article: the Uniform Securitization Scheme which runs invisibly as the operational schematic that underlies all public events be it the birth of a baby, the issuance of currency, economic "bailouts," a Court case, a purchase, a loan, a mortgage or a real estate transaction. Without your awareness, virtually every event of your life which involves a public institution has been covertly superimposed on the underlying Uniform Securitization Scheme ("USS") revealed in this article, so that the actual events are invisible. The USS is the EXACT SAME PROCESS used by banks to PLEDGE your credit card and loan applications as the surety for certificates and notes issued by their subsidiaries and sold to investors. Patriot mythology has held that these loan applications are actually securities. As will be revealed, in this instance the legend is true. The evidence is contained in every Rule 424(b)(5) prospectus filed by every bank with the SEC. A Bank of America flowchart published in a 2010 SEC prospectus is included in Appendix B to graphically demonstrate the universality of the USS. This chilling roadmap to the Uniform Securitization Scam may be helpful to review as you read about the pledges, certification, re-deposit and various techniques that comprise the USS. To understand the Uniform Securities Scheme is to understand the commercial world around you, and the banks, government agencies and Courts that seek to control your life. The author has no objection if a copy of this article is sent to every JUDGE TRUST on the Federal and State benches, and every political prisoner in America.

1. THE UNIFORM SECURITIZATION SCAM: The fuel behind the United States Federal corporation, the underlying premise behind every transaction in which you have participated, is the presumption that your labor has been voluntarily pledged to pay the debts of the United States (the public debt). Is this presumption factual or the wild concoction of misguided conspiracy theorists? Is it even remotely possible that the Founders' descendants are captured as sureties for the escapades of their public officials? The answer will soon be clear. It will be found by exploring a series of legal maneuvers known as "legalization," registration, certification, securitization and general deposit which comprise the essence of the Uniform Securitization Scheme ("USS"). That same scheme is used at every stage of the Matrix, from the construction of the birth account to the reverse mortgage you sign on your death bed. To understand the birth certificate scam, is to understand loans, mortgages, purchases, deeds and all the other mirror-image substitutions for good old fashioned truth.

II THE PLEDGE OF FUTURE PEREORMANCE; SECURITY FUTURES Almost immediately, the blessed event of the delivery of an infant is marred by using its right foot to make an impression on a hospital birth record (HER). The HER provides public testimony of the baby's "birth" on the continent and status as an "owner" of the United States. Contrary to popular opinion, ownership is not control. In the "legal" system, ownership is defined as a pledge to act as surety for the debts incurred by the property. In the case of the United States, that doctrine is enshrined in Article VI of the Constitution which says: "All Debts contracted and Engagements entered into, before the Adoption of this Constitution, shall be as valid against the United States under this Constitution, as under the Confederation." In other words, the act of registering the child with the United States Federal corporation through a government-licensed hospital comprises THE OWNER'S PLEDGE OF FUTURE LAEOR, the "full faith and credit" that underwrites all U.S. currency and public debt under the ancient doctrine that ownership equals liability . After all, who else but the owners would be motivated to pay the bills? For the sake of skeptical friends and family, here are the sound bites: Who else but the people of the United States stand behind U.S. currency? Does the issuance of a U.S. hospital birth record signify one's responsibility to pay taxes and underwrite the public debt?

Ill OPENING AN ACCOUNT: The HER is delivered to the incorporated County for the purpose of transmitting the infant's pledge into the "legal" system. What happens when you transfer property? What must you do when you make a purchase on the internet? What's the first step in creating a commercial relationship with your doctor, bank and phone company? They open an account in your name. As with any asset, the incorporate County as the receiving institution must open an account and log it in. The County Registrar opens an account in the County's books. As you will discover, the sole purpose of every account that has ever been opened in your name is to leverage (issue) future securities. You are unaware of this because you are unaware of the definition of securities. Opening an account is a boilerplate event in the Uniform Securitization Scam when any bank. Court, corporation or government institution seeks to assess the owner with a portion of the public debt and tap into your Estate to pay the assessment.

IV REDUCING STATUS TO A NUMBER: As with any account, the County birth account is assigned a number, typically in the format: 123-45-654321. The first number group identifies the corporate State, the second group identifies the year of delivery, and the third group identifies the transaction. This birth identification number will follow the infant throughout his life. The implications are well documented in Scripture. "And Satan stood up against Israel, and provoked David to number Israel (1 Chronicles 21:1)." You may wish to read about the consequences of that event to the people of Israel. When we participate in a census for purposes other than to glorify the Lord, we can expect to be condemned.

V RECORDING A GENERAL DEPOSIT; RELINQUISHING TITLE: The registrar then records the HBR in the account as a general deposit, meaning the State takes title to the funds (your future labor/commercial energy) the same way a bank takes title to your deposits when you use the bank's endorsement stamp to print "PAY TO THE ORDER OF ACME BANK" on the back of a check before depositing it in "your" account. Haven't you ever wondered why checks are made payable to the bank instead of to your account? The PAY TO THE ORDER OF notation is not just a material alteration under the Uniform Commercial Code. It creates a brand new security wherein the bank takes your funds for its own purposes and disguises the acquisition by issuing credits to your account. This one act is the mechanism by which the

State steals the infant's Divine right to her own labor and converts it into a numbered account to act as surety for it's portion of the public debt owed to the banking cartels under the Constitution. The United States now holds the pledge of the minor child's future labor deposited "voluntarily" by the child's mother as the foundation for all the future securities it will attempt to issue in your name . The HBR is then placed into a vault at City Hall or the County Seat or a subsidiary such as Vital Records. Those who are skeptical might wish to examine their own birth certificates alongside a stock or bond certificate and read the definition of securities in Section 78c of Title 15 of United States Code (subparagraph (a)(10)). The internet provides immediate

access(http://uscode.regstodav.com/15USC CHAPTER2B.aspx#15USC78c) .

VI LEGALIZATION OF YOUR PUBLIC ESTATE

Your estate here on earth consists of your inheritance from the Creator: your body, the air you breath, your possessions, the fruits of your labor. However, as with your name, churches, money, law and courts of record, U.S. Inc. intends to create a fictional mirror-image counterpart of your estate in the public venue. This process is known as "legalization." Depositing your presumed security future pledge into a public account for the creation of securities "legalizes" your labor into a public estate ("Estate"), a vast account which holds the pledge of your future labor (an IOU) to act as surety for your portion of the public debt. Every time your strawman is "charged," the government is seeking to tap into your Estate to pay the assessment. Your Estate is merely a trust which has been designated as insurance to underwrite the public debt and create profits and proceeds for public officials who seek to convert you from a member of the posterity they are sworn to serve into a subject that exists to provide them with commercial energy and position.

VII CERTIFICATION:

The Registrar certifies the deposit of the pledge by issuing a Certificate of Live Birth or Certificate of Birth (so-called long form) which identifies the child, the parents, the date of birth and the date of certification . This one act legalizes the pledge by converting the presumption of pledged labor into a security . Section 8- 102(a)(4) of the Uniform Commercial Code defines a "Certificated Security" as "a security that is represented by a certificate." By issuing the Certificate, the Registrar is confessing that the hospital birth record is a certificated security, and the County is the depository institution which has taken title to the "funds." Certification is the same process used by banks to launder your credit application into an "asset" to be sold to investors. The BOA flowchart in Appendix B provides a graphic confession of the certification scam. Notice that the BA Master Credit Card Trust II is the certificating subsidiary that certificates your credit card application.What is a credit card application? A pledge. It's your pledge (security future) to pay the line-of- credit that the bank "creates" when they approve your credit card application. Regarding general deposit and certification, the County and Bank of America are birds of a feather. Both seek to interpret your signature as a pledge of future performance, a security future . The act of certificating the hospital birth record legalizes the infant's pledge as a security future "asset" for posting as tangible funds in various public accounts as you will see. This is the scheme by which the obligation to perform is transferred from public officials who are sworn to act as trustees of the public trust, to the hapless "legal" Citizen "strawman" created (as you will see later) to act as a substitute trustee through the proess of "legalizing" the infant's pledge into the publicvenue.

VIII REDEPOSIT: The Secretary of the Treasury is notified of the pledge presumably by the transmission of a certified copy of the pledge certificate or electronic record of the County deposit, thereby beginning the Uniform Securitization Scam (create an account, make a general deposit, certificate the "asset," issue derivative securities as if they're tax exempt original issues) once again. The Secretary' delegates open an account identified by the previously assigned birth certificate number for the sole purpose of leveraging (issuing) securities against your Estate. The infant's pledge represented by the Certificate of Live Birth is deposited, again generally, providing the "funds" against which future securities will be issued.THIS IS HOW THE CORPORATION TAPS INTO THE ESTATE TO UNDERWRITE EVERY SECURITY THAT IT ISSUES, every indictment, citation, bill, bond, charging instrument, complaint, summons, arrest warrant, promissory note, assessment and mortgage. THIS IS WHY THE GURUS HAVE TOLD YOU EVERYTHING IS PREPAID. Under the UCC, the term "for value" is defined as a pre-paid account. The birth account at Treasury is the prepaid account against which all such assessments, and your setoffs and acceptances "for value" will be drawn. The pre-payment is the long form Certificate of Live Birth representing the security future pledge of future labor. This is the account that supplies the funds when you mark a bill "charge the same to JOHN HENRY DOE 123-45-6789." This is the elusive "Treasury account" prosecutors love to ridicule when prosecuting a patriot. For many patriots, this may be the first time you have understood what you've been writing in your acceptances. Without this understanding, how could you possibly hope to enforce them? The potential damage to themselves and the technology when thousands of people issue acceptances without adequate understanding of the processes and cheer each other on in Yahoo groups is self- evident.

IX CREATION OF A TRUST: When property is transferred, a trust relationship is created. The recipient has an obligation to perform in some fashion such as processing an instrument, protecting the property or delivering a bill. The recipient is therefore a trustee. Section 401 of the Uniform Trust Code confirms that a trust is created upon transfer of property.

SECTION 401. METHODS OF CREATING TRUST.

A trust may be created by: (I) transfer of property to another person as trustee. . . As with any conveyance of property, the deposit of the pledge creates a trust in which the recipient has a trustee obligation to process the instrument. This is the so-called Birth Certificate trust. It is not the result of some bureaucrat recording a trust, but the natural consequence of a transfer. The birth trust is identified by the original birth number assigned by the County registrar. As you will see, this number represents a variety of accounts, trusts, securities and certificates all derived from the original pledge.

RE-ISSUE OF SECONDARY SECURITIES; THE BIRTH BOND The first security issued from the Treasury account is the birth bond which the United States uses to underwrite its currency. Like the pledge, the birth bond is a certificated book-entry security future, a bet against your future performance, which is re-presented (noticed) into the public by a certificate: the short form Birth Certificate. Like any bond, the birth bond is nothing more than evidence of debt; evidence that the Estate (your labor) is the surety for the infant's portion of the public debt. As you may suspect, the purpose of the birth bond is to leverage more securities using the USS template described in this article. The profiteering begins when the birth bond is traded dollar for dollar for money issued by the Federal Reserve, permitting Treasury to place the money into circulation under the premise that it is backed by the people's "full faith and credit." The bond is transmitted by the Fed to The Depository Trust Company where it is placed into "safe keeping" for the purpose of re-issuing a vast array of derivative securities, each one written against the pledge and designed to elicit your consent for profiteering.

XI REGISTRATION: One of the most seemingly benign cogs in the Uniform Securitization Scam, registration, is the process by which a creditor registers a security interest against the owner . Registration is a pernicious method used to take control of "legalized" property by a genuine or presumed secured party under protection of the "legal" franchise and it's incorporated judiciary. Here are some excerpts from the twelve paragraph operational arrangements published by The Depository Trust Company ("DTC") to govern DTC Direct and Indirect Participants: 1. The Depository Trust Company ("DTC"), New York, NY, will act as securities depository for the securities (the "Securities"). The Securities will be issued as fully-registered securities registered in the name of Cede & Co. (DTC's partnership nominee) or such other name as may be requested by an authorized representative of DTC. 3. Purchases of Securities under the DTC system must be made by or through Direct Participants, which will receive a credit for the Securities on DTC's records . The ownership interest of each actual purchaser of each Security ("Beneficial Owner") is in turn to be recorded on the Direct and Indirect Participants' records. Beneficial Owners will not receive written confirmation from DTC of their purchase . There it is in black and white. The birth bond is "registered" to the benefit of DTC. DTC will not even mention the "Beneficial Owner" — the beneficiary — in its records. By combining the terms "beneficiary" (the sole party with the right to enjoy the fruits of the security) with "owner" (the party that's liable for all of the debts and injuries caused by the security), you have been reduced to the lowest common denominator: an owner. Forget the adjective "Beneficial," you don 't matter at all. Your only right is to order the sale of the security to the next hapless owner. If this is hard to accept, ask yourself who suffers when the value of a stock certificate registered to DTC suddenly falls. The owner. Who pays the margin? The owner. Who sells at a loss? The owner. Who makes a profit on the sale by having locked in its position as holder of the security? The Depository Trust Company. Conversely, as stated by DTC, the Direct Participant (the financial institution that made the deposit, in this case, the Fed) will be credited with the value of the security. This means that DTC will post the birth bond on its books as a credit to the Direct Participant, not you, allowing the Direct Participant to enjoy the increase in net worth, to borrow against the value, to post between 3 and 10 percent of the bond's value to the Direct Participant's reserves thereby allowing the Direct Participant to lend out at least nine times the value of the securities using Y OUR pledge as the source of credit. So while your Estate pays all of the bills assessed against the strawman, the Fed enjoys the value of your pledge. IT IS THROUGH THE BOOK-ENTRIES DESCRIBED IN THIS ARTICLE, IN PARTICULAR THE POSTING OF VALUE IN THE RESERVE ACCOUNTS OF FEDERAL RESERVE BANKS, THAT THE PUBLIC TAPS INTO YOUR ESTATE WITHOUT YOUR KNOWLEDGE. In other words, if a Court wishes to assess your Estate, it deposits the indictment security into an account opened in the name of your strawman, and charges the Estate by issuing an arrest warrant security to bring you in for the purpose of consenting to the assessment. Meanwhile, it is trading against the reserve posting by issuing and trading a Case bond issued from the same account.

XII RE-ISSUE OF SECONDARY SECURITIES; THE SOCIAL SECURITY BOND:

The next security issued by Treasury against the pledge is the master Social Security bond. The purpose of the bond is to create a trust (upon redeposit) which will be used as a vessel to transmit public debt, entice the Estate to act publicly as surety for your portion of the public debt, and transmit funds to the English Crown trust.

XIII OPENING AN ACCOUNT; SOCIAL SECURITY

Following the Uniform Securitization Scam blueprint. Treasury authorizes the opening of an account to receive the Social Security bond for the customary purpose of leveraging securities.

XIV REDUCING STATUS TO A NUMBER; SSN Unlike the birth account maintained by the County and the Secretary of the Treasury, the SSaccount is assigned a new name and number: JOHN HENRY DOE, SSN 123-45-6789 for the purpose of identifying various derivative bonds to be issued from the account against your Estate (your pledge).

XV RECORDING A GENERAL DEPOSIT; RELINQUISHING TITLE TO THE SS BOND

As previously described regarding the birth bond, the master Social Security bond is deposited Page 8 of 14 generally into the SS account.

XVI CREATING A TRUST; SOCIAL SECURITY TRUST

As with any transfer of property, the deposit of the SS bond creates a trust relationship. Over the years, the SS trust, JOHN HENRY SMITH ID # 123-45-6789, has become notorious. But the purpose of the trust is worth repeating; The SS trust will be used as a vessel to transmit public debt, entice the Estate to act publicly as surety for your portion of the public debt, and transmit funds to the English Crown trust. The SS trust is a manifestation of debt. It is debt, and nothing more. Internalizing that understanding is helpful to returning control from public officials to the rightful beneficiary that issued the pledge. The trust directives (the terms of the trust) are all the rules and regulations compiled in United States Code and the Code of Federal Regulations. And guess who is obligated to obey them?...

XVII PRESUMPTIONS:The Social Security trust is the vehicle used by public officials to plunder the Estate. Upon deposit of the Social Security bond, the Department of theTreasury through the Internal Revenue Service is the trustee of record. But the government bank would rather be the beneficiary. In order to presume that the United States is the beneficiary. Treasury presumes that the strawman account is also a trustee of the SS trust with the obligation to perform all of the trustee's duties under the public trust. After you accept offers to operate as the trustee on three occasions, the presumption is fulfilled. From then on, the strawman will be treated as a vehicle for transmitting public debt assessments to the Estate by "charging" the strawman for the liability The stranglehold of the Uniform Securitization Scheme on our lives is BROKEN when we reverse the process and use the SS trust to transmit funds from the Estate to the assessing party upon our express authorization . The name of this process is "setoff."

THE UNIFORM IN UNIFORM Every public transaction mimics the Uniform Securitization Scam. During the $700B bailout of 2008, Treasury issued $700B in bonds, the Fed issued $700B of U.S. money, the bonds were exchanged for the funds and then deposited with DTC following the USS model. When a prosecutor lodges an indictment with a Court, the Court opens an account, the indictment or information is deposited generally, and an arrest warrant is issued against the indictment which is presumed to be backed by the pledge as manifested in the Estate. When an attorney lodges a complaint with a Court, the Court opens an account, the complaint is deposited generally, and a summons is issued against the indictment which is presumed to be backed by the pledge as manifested in the Estate. When you make a withdrawal from at a bank, the bank endorses your draft "PAY TO THE ORDER OF" thereby creating a new security which it posts in its books and exchanges for Federal Reserve Notes, securities of equivalent value.When you issue a mortgage (promissory) note, the bank opens an account, deposits the note generally thereby taking title to the funds, posts it as an asset and offsetting liability at the full value of the note to the bank (which includes the value of all future interest), and issues a bank check to the seller in the lower face value of the note (uneven exchange), thereby leaving a balance owed to the maker which usually goes unclaimed. the purchase of groceries is also a well-disguised exchange of securities. Federal Reserve Notes, a bank draft or a credit card invoice (security futures) for a cash receipt. In the present economic system of credit swaps, the theft of the groceries without providing equal value is ignored. "It's the securities, stupid." All of these transactions are examples of how the USS manifests in our lives.

CHARGING:To "charge" is to draw funds. How does the public levy the Estate to pay an assessment? The answer is right in front of our face. They charge the strawman account 123-45-6789. Might we follow the same approach if we intend to draw the funds for an acceptance from the Estate?: CHARGE THE SAME TO John Henry Smith ID # 123-45-654321 (birth name and # as they appear on the long form Certif. of Birth) or CHARGE THE SAME TO JOHN HENRY SMITH 123-45-6789 (the SS trust as used by the public customarily to transmit debt to the Estate) The latter form more closely mimics the customary business practices of public institutions. Notice, a patriot favorite, the "exemption number:" 123456789, is not mentioned.It is strongly suggested that the reader does NOT consider this an invitation to start issuing acceptances. The contents of this article is merely scratching the surface regarding such transactions.

EXEMPTION NUMBER: When the redemption movement began in the last millennium, our knowledge was considerably less. While we believed that a private account must appear on the books to receive the funds and property that had been confiscated in 1933, the identity of that account was elusive. The exemption number was a convention to represent that account in our paperwork. We now understand that the birth number is universally applied to all accounts, trusts, securities and certificates associated with the infant's pledge of our one true commodity, our future labor. So it appears that the value of the Exemption ID Number has lapsed.

CREDITING:Regarding our setoffs, to "credit" is to apply the funds where desired. If we wish to credit the strawman, we might say; CREDIT THE SAME TO JOHN HENRY SMITH 123-45-6789 If we wish to credit a vendor's account, we might say: CREDIT THE SAME TO ACCOUNT # 123456 We might say; CREDIT THE SAME TO JOHN HENRY SMITH 123-45-6789 FOR FURTHER CREDIT TO ACCOUNT # 123456 Or we might say none of that.

CHARGING AND CREDITING: To specify an entire transaction, we might say: CHARGE THE SAME TO John Henry Smith ID # 123-45-654321 CREDIT THE SAME TO JOHN HENRY SMITH 123-45-6789 CHARGE THE SAME TO JOHN HENRY SMITH 123-45-6789" CREDIT THE SAME TO ACCOUNT # 123456 A creditor might also choose to use none of those statements and simply rely upon our acceptance in the manner of a standard banker's acceptance. It all depends on the circumstances and one's understanding of the accounting. AGAIN, READERS ARE CAUTIONED AGAINST UNDERTAKING BRAIN SURGERY WITHOUT A COMPLETE UNDERSTANDING OF PROCESS, ENFORCEMENT AND THE CONSEQUENCES OF THEIR ACTIONS. DO YOU REALLY WISH TO BECOME ANOTHER STATISTIC WHO LOST THE FAMILY HOME, HAD HER WAGES GARNISHED, OR WOUND UP IN FEDERAL PRISON FOR A COUPLE OE YEARS?

The information in this article took many years and much pain and sacrifice to attain and it ONLY TOLFCHES THE SURFACE regarding the birth scam. I'm but the Father's humble servant in this matter, no more perfect than anyone else. The Reclaim Your Securities Yahoo group reflects the calling I perceived to raise the level of discourse to assist our extraction from commerce and return to the Kingdom. The list of topics regarding offset, do-not-detain status and cashing-out is formidable (see Appendix A). Each could easily be the subject of a college course. I hope the members of the Reclaim Your Securities Group will forgive my shortcomings . They are many. . . . I can't in good conscience give you canned answers or sound bite commerce. Those things are available at other Groups. There are many people willing to encourage you to send out paper and let the chips fall where they may. I have a strong conviction based upon experience that such behavior is an invitation to a Divine correction. In other words, don 't do it.I hear your calls to teach you about security agreements, trusts, the Treasury process and setoffs. The reality proven by this article is that postings and emails are inadequate for even one of those topics, and potentially dangerous. Let's face it, thousands of patriots are more than willing to act boldly and then ask, "What do I do now?" Too often those same people are willing to blame others for their decisions. I wish I could analyze everyone's situations. I wish I could wave a wand and provide instant enlightenment. ALL I CAN DO IS PROVIDE INSIGHT in the hope that I am elevating the dialogue. As I've mentioned, the Yahoo Group was not intended to teach rocket science. Despite your desires, you can NOT paint your way out of the Matrix by the numbers. Fortunately, the patriot community has been blessed. We have been led from the Stone Age by courageous people. We owe them our gratitude. Lynn Meredith, Irwin Schiff, Hartford Van Dyke, Leroy Schweitzer, Roger Elvick, Jack Smith, Winston Shrout, Sam Kennedy, Tom Schultz, David Clarence, Jean Keating and others who provided the plateaus that changed the dialogue. Like me, they are imperfect, but not nearly as flawed as today's new crop of backroom "mentors" who would attempt to hide their own greed by condemning these fine heroes for their mortal mistakes, or just for sport. I am moved by these unique words: "Love your enemies, bless them that curse you, do good to them that hate you, and pray for them which despitefully use you, and persecute you." One thing I CAN provide is assurance that the ongoing discussion of securities, trusts and estates at the Reclaim Your Securities Group will elevate the dialogue once again among patriots and their families and friends, and in time, rattle feudalism to the core. For anything beyond that, you will need to find a competent mentor who passes your gut check. As I've told many of you by email, I know a handful, but nowhere near the number that would be needed to satisfy your needs. I'll keep looking.

Title 18 USC § 1001, often simply referred to as false and misleading statements, makes it a felony to knowingly and willfully: police "application for complaint" using Glossa>fictitious names , complainant known as "julie barrett" is unknown to me.
•Falsify or conceal a material fact in any entry or document; or
•Make oral statements to government officials which are materially false and misleading,
• To an official of the federal government in an investigation or official proceeding.

REQUIREMENT[S] OF FILING A PROPER LAWFUL COMPLAINT:
28 U.S. Code § 1746 - Unsworn declarations under penalty of perjury
Current through Pub. L. 114-38. (See Public Laws for the current Congress.)

• US Code

- Notes
- Authorities (CFR)

prev | next

Wherever, under any law of the United States or under any rule, regulation, order, or requirement made pursuant to law, any matter is required or permitted to be supported, evidenced, established, or proved by the sworn declaration, verification, certificate, statement, oath, or affidavit, in writing of the person making the same (other than a deposition, or an oath of office, or an oath required to be taken before a specified official other than a notary public), such matter may, with like force and effect, be supported, evidenced, established, or proved by the unsworn declaration, certificate, verification, or statement, in writing of such person which is subscribed by him, as true under penalty of perjury, and dated, in substantially the following form:

(1)

If executed without the United States: "I declare (or certify, verify, or state) under penalty of perjury under the laws of the United States of America that the foregoing is true and correct. Executed on (date).

(Signature)".

(2)

If executed within the United States, its territories, possessions, or commonwealths: "I declare (or certify, verify, or state) under penalty of perjury that the foregoing is true and correct. Executed on (date).

(Signature)".

157 South Street
P.O.Box 1718
Plainville, MA 02762
508-699-1212

Incident Report

Narrative by: Sergeant Scott Gallerani   Division: Patrol Personnel (continued)

INCIDENT REPORTED DATE/TIME: 11/6/2009 8:45:07PM

THE FOLLOWING MAY OR MAY NOT BE ALL THE INFORMATION KNOWN TO THE PLAINVILLE POLICE DEPARTMENT.
ALL ROADS MENTIONED HEREIN ARE PUBLIC WAYS IN THE TOWN OF PLAINVILLE UNLESS OTHERWISE NOTED.

was confirmed as RI 54329, a white Chevy Pickup.

I observed a single male occupant not wearing a seat belt looking at paperwork he was taking from his driver's side visor. I observed him for a minute or two before knocking on the window. The male made some hand gestures in my directions, then continued to look through some papers. I then asked the male to roll down the window. He looked in my direction, then slowly reached over to the window to roll it down. He took almost 3 minutes to roll the window down about halfway.

I spoke to the operator and asked for his license and registration. I immediately detected a strong odor of alcohol emanating from within the pickup. The operator's eyes were extremely bloodshot, and he had trouble keeping them open. His speech was slurred when he spoke, and all of his movements were very slow and deliberate. I asked the operator where he was heading, and he said, "Hartford." I asked where he was coming from, and he said, "Rhode Island." I informed the operator the reason for the stop, that he was observed driving erratically.

The operator asked if he could exit his vehicle to retrieve his license from his wallet. I advised him he could, and informed Ptl. Holbrook, who was near the rear of the pickup, that the operator would be exiting. The male stepped out of the pickup, and immediately braced himself against his pickup to avoid falling. Ptl. Holbrook grabbed the operator's right arm to assist with steadying him. He was then escorted to the rear of the pickup. When he got to the rear of the pickup, he fell against the back of it.

The operator pulled several papers out of his right rear pocket (no wallet). He went through the pile twice, and eventually found his driver's license, which identified him as Troy SUMAL, 5/17/1966, of Warwick, RI. I asked SUMAL how much he had to drink, and SUMAL began saying, "Oh I know how this works. You're gonna tow my truck, I have to pay $30 to get it out, I'm gonna go to jail..." I asked SUMAL why he thought he was going to jail. He said, "Because I drove into the wrong lane without signaling." I informed him that that was not a reason to arrest someone. I told SUMAL that I would like to conduct some tests to determine if he would be able to continue driving. I asked SUMAL about his education level, and he replied, "More than you."

I asked SUMAL again if he would like to take some tests, and he began talking about his left arm, which he claimed was permanently disabled. I told him that his arm would not be subject to any testing. SUMAL continually tried to change the subject and not take any tests. During this conversation, SUMAL continually leaned on his pickup, and his eyes were half closed for much of the time. His speech was slurred, and the odor of alcohol emanating from his breath was strong, even in the outdoor air.

Based on the original call for the erratic operation, my observation of operation, Ptl. Holbrook's and my further investigation and observation of SUMAL's bloodshot eyes, slurred speech, strong odor of alcohol, and difficulty standing, SUMAL was placed under arrest for OUI. He was handcuffed (d/l), searched, and placed in cruiser 304. T & D was contacted to tow the vehicle. An inventory of the vehicle revealed a 750 ml of Popov Vodka in a paper bag on the front seat of the vehicle. The bottle was more than half empty. The inventory was completed and T & D removed the vehicle.
The inspection sticker was examined, and it had expired 10/2009. The windshield was also cracked.

SUMAL was transported to the station house, booked, advised of all rights, and photographed. Ptl. Rockett booked SUMAL, while Sgt. Gallerani observed him. The observation period began at 21:32. As Ptl. Rockett was asking the standard booking questions, SUMAL refused to answer any questions, stating, "I plead the fifth." We attempted to explain the chemical test and its consequences, but SUMAL refused to listen and told us that he knew his rights and was pleading the fifth. I asked him if he knew what pleading the fifth was, and he said, "Freedom of Speech!" He was advised that he was being given a refusal for the chemical test. SUMAL continued to proclaim his knowledge of the law. He was then placed in cell 2, and advised that a phone call could be made from the phone in the cell. He was also advised that his property would be inventoried.

A check of SUMAL's criminal history reveals two prior OUI's, one in Florida (Lee County Sheriff's Office 11/4/1995), and another in Tennessee (Crossville Sheriff's Office 9/23/2000).

NEVER CONVICTED!!

Plainville Police Department
157 South Street
P.O.Box 1718
Plainville, MA 02762
508-699-1212

Incident Number: 2009000007271
Dispatch Incident Number: 2009000002621
Print Date: November 7, 2009

Incident Report

| Narrative by: Sergeant Scott Gallerani   Division: Patrol Personnel (continued) |

INCIDENT REPORTED DATE/TIME: 11/6/2009 8:45:07PM

THE FOLLOWING MAY OR MAY NOT BE ALL THE INFORMATION KNOWN TO THE PLAINVILLE POLICE DEPARTMENT.
ALL ROADS MENTIONED HEREIN ARE PUBLIC WAYS IN THE TOWN OF PLAINVILLE UNLESS OTHERWISE NOTED.

As a result of this complaint, traffic stop, and subsequent investigation, Troy SUMAL was issued citations M7258102, M7258103, and M7258104 for:

90.24 Operating Under the Influence of Liquor - 3rd Offense
90.24 Negligent Operation of a Motor Vehicle
90.24I Open Container
89.4A Marked Lanes Violation
90.13A Seat Belt Violation
90.20 No Inspection Sticker
90.7 Defective Equipment (windshield)
90.11 No Reg. in Possession

[handwritten: ↑ FRAUD Grammar!]

Incident Notes:

| Create User ID: |

Date & Time
No Incident Notes Listed

Incident Number: 2009000007271
Dispatch Incident Number: 2009000002621
Print Date: November 7, 2009

Incident Report

Incident Information

Occurred On/From	Day of Week	Date	Time	Occurred To	Day of Week	Date	Time	Reported On	Date	Time
	Fri	11/06/2009	8:45:00PM		Fri	11/06/2009	8:45:00PM	→	11/6/2009	8:45:07PM

Reported As	Incident Type - Primary	Arresting Officer
Traffic Complaint	Operating M/V Intoxicated	Sergeant Scott Gallerani

Incident Address	Reporting Officer
WASHINGTON ST, PLAINVILLE, MA 02762	Sergeant Scott Gallerani

Business Name	Incident Types : Other
N/A	Traffic Complaint

Associated Persons Summary

Type	Name(Last, First, MI)	Date of Birth	Sex	Home Phone #	Cell Phone #	Work Phone #
Arrested	Sumal, Troy J.	5/17/1966	M	N/A	N/A	N/A
Address:	199 Cottage Grove Dr., Warwick, RI 02888					
					N/A	N/A
Address:						

Associated Businesses Summary

Type	Name	Primary Phone #	Secondary Phone #
No Associated Persons reported for Incident #: 2009000007271			

Vehicle Info

Vehicle No.	Vehicle Make	Vehicle Model	Vehicle Year	VIN	Primary Color	Secondary Color	Plate No.	State
2009000002455	Chevrolet	N/A	1994	1GCFC24H2RE181602	White	N/A	54329	RI

Narrative by: Sergeant Scott Gallerani   Division: Patrol Personnel

INCIDENT REPORTED DATE/TIME: 11/6/2009 8:45:07PM

THE FOLLOWING MAY OR MAY NOT BE ALL THE INFORMATION KNOWN TO THE PLAINVILLE POLICE DEPARTMENT. ALL ROADS MENTIONED HEREIN ARE PUBLIC WAYS IN THE TOWN OF PLAINVILLE UNLESS OTHERWISE NOTED.

On November 6, 2009 at about 20:45, the station house received a 911 cell phone call from a female stating that she and her husband were driving behind a suspected drunk driver. The caller stated that she and her husband were travelling northbound on Rt. 1 (Washington St). Rt. 1 is a public way in the town of Plainville. They had observed the vehicle, a White Chevy Pickup with a cap on it, on the median in North Attleboro. The plate given was RI 54329.

The caller followed behind the vehicle as it entered Plainville and continued northbound on Rt. 1. Sgt. Gallerani and Ptl. Holbrook were dispatched to the call as the vehicle was passing Osborne Nursery on Rt. 1. The caller gave continual updates of the location. Dispatcher Rando advised the caller to turn on their four way flashers (hazard lights) to identify their vehicle so the officers could locate the suspect vehicle easier. The caller stated that the pickup almost struck the guardrail just north of the Tavern. The caller then stated that the pickup was in the left hand lane, and nearly struck a vehicle head-on travelling southbound on Rt. 1.

The officers continued northbound with emergency lights activated and located the pickup truck as it entered the on-ramp to Rt. 495 southbound. I, Sgt. Gallerani observed the pickup fail to signal as it entered the ramp, then nearly strike the curbing on the left side of the ramp. I was directly behind the pickup and turned my cruiser's siren on. The pickup slowed to a crawl, and travelled for another 30-40 feet before stopping. I advised dispatch of the location, and approached the pickup from the passenger side. The vehicle's plate

APPLICATION FOR CRIMINAL COMPLAINT

APPLICATION NO. (COURT USE ONLY)	PAGE
09-3036	3 of 3

Trial Court of Massachusetts
District Court Department

WRENTHAM DISTRICT COURT
60 EAST ST.
WRENTHAM MA 02093

I, the undersigned complainant, request that a criminal complaint issue against the accused charging the offense(s) listed below. If the accused **HAS NOT BEEN ARRESTED** and the charges involve:

☐ ONLY MISDEMEANOR(S), I request a hearing ☐ WITHOUT NOTICE because of an imminent threat of
☐ BODILY INJURY ☐ COMMISSION OF A CRIME ☐ FLIGHT ☐ WITH NOTICE to accused
☐ ONE OR MORE FELONIES, I request a hearing ☐ WITHOUT NOTICE ☐ WITH NOTICE to accused

☐ WARRANT is requested because prosecutor represents that accused may not appear unless arrested.

ARREST STATUS OF ACCUSED
☒ HAS ☐ HAS NOT been arrested

INFORMATION ABOUT ACCUSED

NAME (FIRST MI LAST) AND ADDRESS		
Troy J. Sumal 199 Cottage Grove Dr., Warwick RI, 02888	RECEIVED WRENTHAM DISTRICT COURT CLERK MAGISTRATE	

BIRTH DATE	SOCIAL SECURITY NUMBER
PCF NO. None	MARITAL STATUS
DRIVERS LICENSE NO. 2302500	STATE RI
GENDER Male	HEIGHT 6' 2"	WEIGHT 193	EYES Hazel

HAIR Brown	RACE Caucasian	COMPLEXION Fair	SCARS/MARKS/TATTOOS

BIRTH STATE OR COUNTRY NJ | DAY PHONE

EMPLOYER/SCHOOL Employer: Self-employed	MOTHER'S MAIDEN NAME (FIRST MI LAST) MC: Wilma Yanish NOK:	FATHER'S NAME (FIRST MI LAST) MC: Ronald NOK:

CASE INFORMATION

COMPLAINANT NAME (FIRST MI LAST) Patrol Officer Julie A Barrett	COMPLAINANT TYPE
ADDRESS 157 SOUTH ST, PLAINVILLE MA, 02762	☒ POLICE ☐ CITIZEN ☐ OTHER — Plainville Police Department

PLACE OF OFFENSE
WASHINGTON ST PLAINVILLE MA 02762

INCIDENT REPORT NO. 2009000007271	OBTN TPLV0090000161
CITATION NO(S).	

	OFFENSE CODE	DESCRIPTION	OFFENSE DATE
1	90/7/D	Equipment Violation, Miscellaneous MV	11/06/2009
	VARIABLES (e.g. victim name, controlled substance, type and value of property, other variable information; see Complaint Language Manual)		
2	90/24I	Alcohol From Open Container in MV, Drink	11/06/2009
	VARIABLES		
3	OFFENSE CODE	DESCRIPTION	OFFENSE DATE
	VARIABLES		

REMARKS

COMPLAINANT'S SIGNATURE X _Julie Barrett_ DATE FILED 11-09-09

COURT USE ONLY

A HEARING UPON THIS COMPLAINT APPLICATION WILL BE HELD AT THE ABOVE COURT ADDRESS ON } DATE OF HEARING | TIME OF HEARING | COURT USE ONLY
AT

PROCESSING OF NON-ARREST APPLICATION (COURT USE ONLY) | CLERK/JUDGES

NOTICE SENT OF CLERK'S HEARING SCHEDULED ON:
NOTICE SENT OF JUDGE'S HEARING SCHEDULED ON:
HEARING CONTINUED TO:
APPLICATION DECIDED WITHOUT NOTICE TO ACCUSED BECAUSE:
☐ IMMINENT THREAT OF ☐ BODILY INJURY ☐ CRIME ☐ FLIGHT BY ACCUSED
☐ FELONY CHARGED AND POLICE DO NOT REQUEST NOTICE
☐ FELONY CHARGED BY CIVILIAN: NO NOTICE AT CLERK'S DISCRETION

COMPLAINT TO ISSUE | **COMPLAINT DENIED** | CLERK/JUDGES

DATE 11-9-09

☒ PROBABLE CAUSE FOUND FOR ABOVE OFFENSES
NOS. ☒ 1 ☒ 2 ☐ 3. BASED ON
☐ FACTS SET FORTH IN ATTACHED STATEMENT(S)
☐ TESTIMONY RECORDED: TAPE NO
START NO. END NO.
☐ WARRANT ☒ SUMMONS TO ISSUE
ARRAIGNMENT DATE

COMPLAINT DENIED
☐ NO PROBABLE CAUSE FOUND
☐ REQUEST OF COMPLAINANT
☐ FAILURE TO PROSECUTE
☐ AGREEMENT OF BOTH PARTIES
☐ OTHER:
COMMENT

DCCR-2 (08/04) Booking No. 2009000000161

COURT COPY

ABComplaintSingle 04/20/09

As we can see from the police report, it is clearly a fabrication of lawlessness, how can julie barrett be the "COMPLAINTANT" , ?? and who trained them to use the names the way they do? Without any doubt the BAR taught them, and the BAR protects them !! this is very very sick, and the BAR runs this country right in front of everybody's face they comitt crimes ALL THE TIME and the people cant wake up and take notice of this infestation of rats. A school is call an "indoctrination center" . Can anyone show me a rules and procedure for a "statutory jurisdiction" ? (there are none), And why we werent taught this in school? And who writes the legislature telling the teachers what to teach ? The BAR. Spell your name, sign your name,, nice tricks also,

Crimes/violations:

violation of rights without due process of law,
violation of my personal liberty,
violation of my right to life, liberty, and the persuit of happyness,
false arrest, false imprisonment,
violation of my right to self representation, amendment 6. *25 counts*
violation of my right to a blood or urine test

false personation 18 USC 912 4 counts
conspiracy against rights 18 USC 241, 242.   15 counts
false and misleading statements 18 USC 1001.   15 counts
unsworn statements 12 USC 1746. 4 counts
misapprotiations 18 USC 641 6 counts
no contract[s] in evidence, no full disclosure of multiple jurisdictions
impersonating a public official. 4 counts
cruel and unusual punishment, 20 counts
perjury/lying, about 75 counts
extortion. Unlimited from everybody
Using foreign grammar. 26 counts
Using ex post facto. 5 counts

Ex post facto laws are expressly forbidden by the United States Constitution in Article 1, Section 9, Clause 3 (with respect to federal laws) and Article 1, Section 10
An *ex post facto* law (corrupted from Latin: *ex postfacto*, lit. 'out of the aftermath') is a law that **retroactively changes the legal consequences (or status) of actions that were committed, or relationships that existed,** before the enactment of the law. In criminal law, it may criminalize actions that were legal when committed; it may aggravate a crime by bringing it into a more severe category than it was in when it was committed; it may change the punishment prescribed for a crime, as by adding new penalties or extending sentences; or it may alter the rules of evidence in order to make conviction for a crime likelier than it would have been when the deed was committed. **That means theres no such thing as a "3rd offence" its more bullshit fraud !!**

DAMAGES: 1,000 a day for 10 years plus 17 days =3,669,000 and counting !!(dec 7th 2019 current), +
punative

Well recently the past 5 weeks I had to pawn 2 bicycles for money for living expenses. One bike was a 1986
kuwahara with ARAYA rims in mint condition. Bike was worth 1000$ easily and the pawn shop loaned me
200. that bike is lost now because its been a month and I didnt make a payment. Then I pawned a 1980s
Falcon competitor 600 racing bike with a 531c frame, this was also a rare bike worth about 1500$ but I
could only get 100 for it. Ill probably lose that one too. (both of these bikes I bought at the thrift store, one
was 9.99, and the other 14.99, I cleaned them up and polished the metal. This is how I been surviving is by
buying and selling whatever I can, like vintage modern lighting, small tables made in denmark. Taking these
items on the bus to my storage, but recently theres been a big slump in sales and nothing coming in to the thrift
stores, so its hard times again). I had to sell my 1970s teak coffee taqble made by "stole mobilfabrik" for 150$, it
was worth 675$. I sold my uncirculated kennedy silver half dollars that were all high grade MS63 or better, I
had to take scrap price for them, but if they were graded would have sold for a couple thousand dollars. I sold a
lot of stuff so I could survive>> rather I had to let people steal it from me!!

 This is a tiny tiny fraction of the losses I suffered over the years including hundreds of handyman jobs on
a website called thumbtack I could not do, hundreds of estate sales, auctions, flea markets, my ebay
account still shut down, who knows what life had in store for me. I could have been married by now with a
family, I could be retired,,,,,,,,,,,,,, I do have a very expensive artwork that I cannot bring to boston because
the creeps will lock me up if I go near their territory. Lots of my tools sold and pawned over the years also.
Ive been in several mental facilities because of depression, Ive been baker acted 2 times because I didnt
want to take their pills, the big goons muscled me down to the floor and give me the needle, knocked me
out for over a day because I didnt want to take their psycho pills. There was no counselor with any
answers to this corrupt system and told me their pills will help me feel better, and I told them NO IT
WILL NOT ! I been abused by doctors and police. One time I was arrested for driving with no FL DL,
and the police were so ROTTON AND CRUDE !! absolutely MF SICK DIMENTED SADISTIC EVIL !!!
they had 10 of us in one small cell for 17 hours waiting to go to court, the cell was 40-45 degrees and fans
blowing like a storm !! everybody complained and complained, asking for blankets, asking and
demanding they turn off the fans and AC, during the shift the fat officers would come to the little window
and just look at everyone freezing, (mostly the fat women), and did not have any blankets with him/her, he
just said he'll be back, and then another pig cop came looking in the window and said the same thing, then
they said the next shift would take care of us with blankets or turn off the AC, this never happened and we
were all so angry cussing and swearing all night and next morning. This happened in port charlotte
florida and at least half of them were there for DUI arrests and have not been drinking. One time I had to
sleep on a bare concrete floor and smell the fermented piss in a crowded cell, one other time is so heart-

wrenching im not even going to tell it.

This is why ill never EVER trust a goddam pig again !! theyre all SICKOS.

My truck was towed twice and once sat in a towyard for 45 days and it costed me 1700$ to get it back, another time it costed me 1400$$. all my money gone from going to the flea market(s) selling my merchandise so I could rent a apartment or have $$ to live normally was taken. Ive been homeless numerous times, rented rooms in places I did not want to be, and had to move frequently, missed many showers and had many skin infections from lack of cleanliness. I learned to use rubbing alcohol and wipe myself down now. I dont go to shelters, the only thing I qualify for is a 45 day drug program where they lock you up at the jail annex. Im not on drugs and I prefer not to be around those people. In the mental hospital is no place for me either because I wont take their pills and be treated like a retard. There is no place to go around here. Ive missed many many meals over the years, some days not eating at all. my diet is still not considered even ½ of "proper" today. Still struggling. All jobs that I applied for in the past have required your own transportation so that leaves me out. I get food stamps but its not enough, When I tell these clerks or district attorney on the phone what I am suffering, they are absolutely emotionless and persist in breaking the law because they want their bond(s) money $$$$. I figure 8 charges with a 3rd offence DUI pays out big big money for them Mfs. I've lost friends over this driver lisence scandal and 2 girlfriends couldnt deal with it either>>the>>BS, they just cant keep holding on,,,,,,,,,,and they cant understand WHY wont they talk to me on the phone and WHY do they not respond by mail and why does this continue year after year with no remedy ? And especially now when the statute of limitations expired on nov 9 2015 this is absolutely crazy !!!. one friend is waiting for 8 years for me to go fishing with him. I have no social life, no holidays, no dating, no church, no going anywhere. No life but the scummy bus stop experiences with beggars and druggies begging me for stuff. Theres no decent person wants anything to do with me seeing me walking on the streets with my suitcase. I must have spent over 4000$ on printouts and copies, plus all the registered mail. 15-25,000 hours of research at least. AND THEY ARE THE CRIMINALS !!! I HAVE THE PROOF. They have nothing on me, absolutely nothing !!! presumptions and an offer to contract using extortion.

The reality is that the American people, as individuals, have lost their courage. The government prefers it that way as a fearful people are easier to rule than a courageous one. But Americans don't wish to lose their self-image of courage. So, when confronted with a situation demanding courage, in the form of a government gone wrong, the American people simply pretend that the situation does not exist.

When the World Trade Towers collapsed, most Americans simply refused to believe suggestions that the attacks had been staged by parties working for the US Government itself. Americans were afraid to, even as news reports surfaced proving that the US Government had announced plans for the invasion of Afghanistan early in the year, plans into which the attacks on the World Trade Towers which angered the American people into support of the already-planned war fit entirely too conveniently. But so trapped are Americans by their belief in their own bravery that they will themselves to be blind to the evidence before their eyes, so that they can nod in agreement with the government while still imagining themselves to have courage, even as they avoid the one situation which most requires real courage: to stand up to the government's lies and deceptions. The vast majority of the American people, their own self-image dependent on continuing blindness to the government's deceptions, never question why Afghanistan would have done something so stupid as to attack the United States, and as a result, **Americans find themselves in a war, as deceitful and of the same order of magnitude as the wars of Adolph Hitler in the invasions of the countries of Europe and Africa.**

Now the US Government has requested temporary extraordinary powers, powers specifically banned under Constitutional law, but powers the government is claiming they need to have to deal with the "terrorists". The American people, having already sold their souls to their self-delusions, are agreeing. The temporary powers recently conferred will be no more temporary in America than they were in Germany. **The United States is now in full blown state of Americanized National Socialism. The 4th Reich is firmly established, jackboots, SWAT teams and all.**

The US Government knows they rule a nation of cowards. The government has had to spend the money to make the new war something cowards can fight. The government has decorated the troops with regalia to make them proud of themselves, further trapping them in their self-image. Talismans are added from orthodox religions and the occult to fill the soldiers with delusions of mystical strengths and an afterlife if they fall in battle. Finally, knowing that it takes courage to kill the enemy face to face, the United States government has spent vast sums of money on wonder weapons, airplanes, submarines, ultra-long range artillery, cruise missiles, and guided missiles, weapons that kill at a distance, so that those doing the killing need not have to face the reality of what they are doing.

THE-END,,,,,,,,,,,,,,,,,,,,,,,,,,,, for now